D1648289

"In this lucid, accessible book, Kathlee[...] and lasting value of praying the Psalm[...] describes the formative power of the [...] faith and to sharpen our perception o[...] world. This book promises to inspire those beginning their journey with the Psalms, as well as to spark renewed vitality for life-long worshipers."

> John D. Witvliet, Director, Calvin Institute of Christian Worship
> Professor of Worship, Calvin College and Calvin Theological
> Seminary

"Kathleen Harmon has given us a look at the psalms that is simultaneously inspiring and informative. She shows us from several perspectives how the psalms shape who we are, both individually and communally, and we are led to realize how we need both lament and praise. Her book makes us want to steep ourselves in the spirituality of these prayer-poems and truly 'become the psalms.' The last chapter alone makes the book worth having."

> Irene Nowell, OSB, Adjunct Professor of Theology,
> St. John's University School of Theology

"In *Becoming the Psalms: A Spirituality of Singing and Praying the Psalms*, Kathleen Harmon, SNDdeN, artfully combines solid scriptural scholarship about the psalter with a theological-liturgical grounding, and pragmatic insight drawn from years of experience as a teacher and singing liturgical minister. The book delves deeply into the psalter in a number of ways, though always through a language that will be accessible to most readers. In particular, she is to be congratulated for taking on texts from the psalter that may be difficult for those who have to proclaim or hear them; for addressing the need to keep praying even when God seems silent; and—most importantly—for concluding with our need to live out these rich, ancient texts daily, as disciples. This volume will be a first-rate addition to the bookshelf of anyone involved in liturgical music ministry, scripture study, preaching, or spirituality."

> Alan J. Hommerding
> Senior Liturgy Publications Editor
> World Library Publications

Becoming the Psalms

A Spirituality of Singing
and Praying the Psalms

Kathleen Harmon

LITURGICAL PRESS
Collegeville, Minnesota

www.litpress.org

1   2   3   4   5   6   7   8   9

Library of Congress Cataloging-in-Publication Data

Harmon, Kathleen A., 1944–
    Becoming the Psalms : a spirituality of singing and praying the Psalms
/ Kathleen Harmon.
       pages cm
    ISBN 978-0-8146-4859-9 — ISBN 978-0-8146-4884-1 (ebook)
    1. Bible. Psalms—Devotional use.   2. Spiritual life—Catholic Church.
I. Title.

BS1430.54.H37   2015
223'.206—dc23   2015001558

Contents

Introduction

Joseph Gelineau, the influential Scripture scholar, liturgist, and musician, once wrote that a person who prays the psalms "becomes for God one of God's own psalms."[1] His statement implies that a psalm has ontological import: it *effects* who we are, bringing us into being in some way. We can never exhaust the significance this insight carries for the community of the church who prays psalms on a daily basis. Why do we pray these texts composed so many years ago over the course of another faith tradition's long history? What is the power these texts carry, even today for a church alive in another time, another culture, another historical situation? The answer, of course, is that Israel's story is the church's story. The psalms are a poetic, prayer-filled form of telling this story. Each time we tell it, each time we hear it, each time we sing it, we enter anew into its drama and recognize it as our own. We recognize that this is a story of faith arrived at only haltingly by a people who wrestled tirelessly and tiresomely with a God whose every intervention was directed toward their salvation. We enter the drama's twists and turns, its painful self-confrontation and its hope-filled orientation, in order to surrender ourselves to its transforming process.

We all know the power of praying a particular psalm when caught up in a spiritual, psychological, or physical crisis. In the midst of grief, for example, praying Psalm 23 reassures us of God's tender and attentive care for us, even in the face of death. When uncertain

---

[1] Joseph Gelineau, "The Concrete Forms of Common Prayer," *Studia Liturgica* 10 (1974): 144.

of our personal value, praying Psalm 139 reinstates our sense of worth as one intimately known and knit together by God in our mother's womb. But the praying of the psalms also calls for a wider "reading." We must pray the psalms in the context of the whole story of Israel's faith journey, in the context of the church's faith journey, and in the context of the journey of all of humankind to salvation. As these "readings" interact, new meanings emerge within the psalms, new faith possibilities arise, and we tap into the extraordinary and limitless theological depths of these prayers.

This book, an edited and expanded collection of several of my Music Notes columns from *Liturgical Ministry*, delves into the phenomenon of what it means for us as the church to pray the psalms, why we must pray these texts, and who we become as we do so. My hope in sharing these essays is that readers will come to recognize what these texts, inspired by God and derived from human suffering and human joy, *do* to us when we pray them.

Whether our praying of a psalm is private or communal, spoken or sung, the psalm is not a neutral text, but a profoundly formative one. What is being formed? How is it being formed? What does it mean to *become* the psalm? Part of the answer lies in knowing that the psalms are the story of salvation told in the form of poetic prayers. Another part lies in recognizing that this story, these prayers are ours. A final part lies in letting the story of salvation mold our everyday thinking and living.

That is what this present book is about.

PART I

The Psalms,
the Story of Salvation

The psalms are a poetic version of the story of salvation, a nutshell retelling of the entire content of the Scriptures. In the following chapters, we examine how the Hebrew Psalter was edited and structured to tell this story, to point where it leads, and to reveal the hills and valleys God's people would traverse as they moved along its path. We reflect on the role Psalm 1 plays in the Psalter, on its language and imagery, its relationship to Psalm 150, and its significance for us today as we choose to walk faithfully in the way of God.

The story of salvation is the narrative of God's ongoing work to bring humanity "to its senses," so to speak, to lead us to see who we truly are and how we are to act. It is the ongoing story of our slipping and sliding away from the truth, and God acting to nudge us back, sometimes gently, other times with a mighty kick. It is the story of a Love that chooses death so we might live. And it is finally the story of our choosing to love in that same way. When we pray the psalms, whether alone or with the church gathered for liturgy, we enter into the story of salvation as it is unfolding here and now, in this day and age, at this very moment. The story becomes ours, and we become its participants. Even more, we become its song.

The Story Told by the Psalms

The Content of the Psalms

The collection of 150 psalms in the Hebrew Scriptures is divided into five books (scholars speculate this division is deliberately patterned after the Pentateuch): Psalms 1–41, 42–72, 73–89, 90–106, and 107–50. The concluding psalm of each book closes with some form of the acclamation "Blessed be God!" (variably rendered "Praise the Lord!" or "Alleluia!").

> Blessed be the LORD, the God of Israel,
>> from all eternity and forever.
>> Amen. Amen. (Ps 41:14)[1]

> Blessed be the LORD, the God of Israel,
>> who alone does wonderful deeds.
> Blessed be [God's] glorious name forever;
>> may all the earth be filled with the LORD's glory.
> Amen and amen. (Ps 72:18-19)

> Blessed be the LORD forever! Amen and amen! (Ps 89:53)
> Blessed be the LORD, the God of Israel,
>> from everlasting to everlasting!
>> Let all the people say, Amen!
> Hallelujah! (Ps 106:48)

---

[1] Psalm verses in this chapter are taken from the NAB, with adaptations by the author for inclusive language.

The conclusion of the fifth book is actually a series of five psalms (146–50), each beginning and ending with "Praise the Lord!" The grand finale, Psalm 150, is built completely around this shout of praise:

> Hallelujah!
>
> Praise God in his holy sanctuary;
>   give praise in the mighty dome of heaven.
> Give praise for [God's] mighty deeds,
>   praise [God] for his great majesty.
> Give praise with blasts upon the horn,
>   praise [God] with harp and lyre.
> Give praise with tambourines and dance,
>   praise [God] with flutes and strings.
> Give praise with crashing cymbals,
>   praise [God] with sounding cymbals.
> Let everything that has breath
>   give praise to the LORD!
> Hallelujah!

The Hebrew Psalter is, then, a series of five books each ending with "Praise the Lord!," with a concluding "chapter" of five psalms each framed by "Praise the Lord!," and a grand finale of crescendo-ing Alleluias in Psalm 150. Between Psalm 1 and Psalms 146–50, the Psalter relates the entire story of salvation in all its ups and downs: lament, grief, revenge, anger, joy, restoration, thanksgiving, praise, sin, forgiveness, suffering, release, loss, defeat, victory, sorrow, danger, despair, hope. Every possible human experience, human emotion, human outcry is expressed, all of it moving ineluctably toward praise of the God who saves.

What the psalms do is express in terms of human experience the nature of the interaction between us and God. From the human side this is a continual movement between lament and praise, sin and forgiveness, suffering and release. From the divine side it is a story of steadfast love, enduring compassion, and rectifying justice. It is the ongoing story of our wailing to be saved and our rejoicing when we are, and of our discovery that God is at the bottom of both the wailing and the rejoicing.

This brings us to a second point about the nature of the psalms: they are at one and the same time human cries and divine word. All of Scripture is the word of God, but the psalms—alone of Scripture—are also human prayers. They are different from all other scriptural texts. Though they include historical references, they are not historical records; though they include a great deal of theology and teaching, they are not theological treatises; though they speak of the law and the consequences of following or not following it, they are not legal documents. The psalms are prayers, individual and communal.[2] They are human cries that are God's word, and in praying them we become who we are: the people molded by the story begun and completed by God.

The Psalms as Our Story

The more we pray the psalms, the more we discover that they are a communal diary with intimately personal footnotes. As Scripture scholar and musician Irene Nowell, OSB, once noted, "There's nothing in the psalms that's not in my own journal. The only difference is that in my journal there are names attached."

To pray the psalms with understanding, then, we must be aware of what our own story of salvation is. For example, there are ways that God has acted in us to change fear into freedom, coldness into warmth, sin into reconciliation. There are ways that God has acted to nudge us from doubt to deeper faith, from defensiveness to openness, from hesitation to willingness to run risks for the kingdom. There are ways that God has transformed our interpersonal conflicts into experiences of compassion, understanding, and forgiveness. There are ways that God has moved us from isolation and self-centeredness to a sense of community with others—with

---

[2] "The key to using psalms is to remember that they are first person speech to God. . . . The most frequent misuse of the Psalms is to treat their secondary uses—as history, theology, wisdom—as primary. The psalms are primarily prayer, speech to God" (Terry Muck, "Psalm, *Bhajan*, and *Kirtan*: Songs of the Soul in Comparative Perspective," in *Psalms and Practice: Worship, Virtue, and Authority*, ed. Stephen Breck Reid, 9 [Collegeville, MN: Liturgical Press, 2001]).

the church, with the stranger on the street, with the whole world community.

All of these experiences are movements initiated and supported by the God who acts always on behalf of our redemption. They are the ways that God reaches down into the painful stuff of our lives—the angers and fears, the losses and griefs, the sins and re-bellions—and pulls us out. They are real-life, everyday fulfillments of God's promise of salvation. The more consciously we can name these experiences of God's saving activity, the more sense the psalms will make to us, for we begin to see that they are a chronicle of the action taking place in our lives, and of Who it is that is acting.

Furthermore, we discover that the chronicle is a communal one. Many psalms were written for communal use in Jewish liturgical celebrations. But even the psalms written in first person singular and prayed alone were never individualized in the Jewish mind. The very capacity to pray them arose from the individual's sense of being a member of God's chosen people. For the Jewish community, all of life was worship, and worship entailed acknowledging their relatedness to one another and living accordingly. The psalms arose out of the context of the salvation story of the whole people. We, too, march toward redemption as a community, our stories part and parcel of one another. Praying the psalms leads us to see more and more clearly that every person's suffering, every person's cry of lament, every person's release, every person's cry of praise, is our own.

From the Beginning to the End

Walking the Way toward Praise of God

Psalm 1

Scholars generally agree that Psalm 1 was deliberately composed after the Hebrew Psalter had been edited into its present form sometime during the late sixth century BCE.[1] Psalm 1 stands as the introduction to the entire collection and sets a direction not only for the progression of the psalms that follow but also for the progression of a righteous person's life:

> Blessed is the one
> > who does not walk in step with the wicked
> or stand in the way that sinners take
> > or sit in the company of mockers,
> but whose delight is in the law of the LORD,
> > and who meditates on his law day and night.
> That person is like a tree planted by streams of water,
> > which yields its fruit in season
> and whose leaf does not wither—
> > whatever they do prospers.

---

[1] Psalm 1 pairs with Psalm 2 as a deliberate introduction to the Hebrew Psalter, Psalm 1 dealing with *tōrah*, or the way of God, and Psalm 2 dealing with messiah, the anointed one of God.

Not so the wicked!
    They are like chaff
    that the wind blows away.
Therefore the wicked will not stand in the judgment,
    nor sinners in the assembly of the righteous.

For the LORD watches over the way of the righteous,
    but the way of the wicked leads to destruction.[2]

At first glance, Psalm 1 seems an easy read. Two strophes contrast the way of the righteous with the way of the wicked. The instruction is clear: walk in the way of God and you will live; follow the way of wickedness and you will die. But examination of the psalm's language and imagery reveals a complex poetic text rich in nuance, implied warning, and eschatological promise.

Language and Imagery in Psalm 1

Our ability to enter into the teaching of Psalm 1 hinges on our grasping the meaning of several terms that carry a very different sense in Hebrew from the way we commonly use these terms in English. We have some translation work to do.

To begin with, the word "blessed" (Heb. *ashrē*) does not carry the static connotation we often give it. *Ashrē* derives from a root meaning "to go forward," "to walk on," "to march steadily."[3] Blessed is not a state of being, then, but a journey toward becoming, a "doing in the making." The blessed do not stay in place but walk on a "way" (Heb. *derek*) that demands repeated choice and steadfast perseverance. The journey is a time-bound, here and now, "day and night" (v. 2) endeavor on our part. Yet we do not control the moment of our arrival at the journey's destination. We will bear fruit not at a time of our choosing, but when the "season" comes (v. 3). The wicked will meet their timely end on the day of judgment

---

[2] Psalm verses in this chapter are taken from the NIV.

[3] Samuel Terrien, *The Psalms: Strophic Structure and Theological Commentary* (Grand Rapids, MI: William B. Eerdmans, 2003), 71.

(v. 5), but no one knows when that day will come. One of the implications of Psalm 1, then, is that we do not know how long the journey will be, how long our becoming will take. As subsequent psalms will reveal, we must trudge on through dark days and terrifying nights, surrounded by evil and confronted by opposition. We can only do so because we know that God "watches over the way of the righteous" (v. 6) and that God's judgment of the wicked will come at its appointed time.

Another central image in Psalm 1 is the "way" (Heb. *derek*). The word *derek* is used extensively in biblical literature, appearing 706 times in the Hebrew testament alone. There are two ways we can follow. We can choose the way of sinners, becoming progressively more aligned with them as we "walk" with them, "stand" by them, and eventually "sit" down in their midst (v. 1). Or we can choose the "way of the righteous" (v. 6) who meditate every moment on the "law of the LORD" (v. 2). Such meditating is an integral part of the way because it is the internal catalyst of our movement forward. In Hebrew the word meditate (*hāghāh*) refers to a type of muttering or moaning, a ceaseless whispering of God's word in a manner that is quiet yet also audible. To meditate on God's law, then, is to make that law the driving voice in our hearts and minds. It is also to make God's law heard in our way of living and acting.

This law (Heb. *tōrah*) upon which we meditate is not an inhibiting legalism shackling our freedom, as we tend to think with our Western mindset. Rather, *tōrah* refers to the will and purpose of God as that has been "ordained in the very structure of life."[4] It means God's "way," the divine *derek* revealed in every fiber of the natural world, in every loving human relationship, in every healthy human community. It is encoded in the first five books of the Bible, which tell the story of God's ceaseless action to form a people and lead them into a future fraught with freedom and fullness of life. It encompasses the obligations of lifestyle incumbent upon this people

---

[4] Walter Brueggemann, *The Message of the Psalms: A Theological Commentary* (Minneapolis: Augsburg, 1984), 38.

who tell and retell this story of God's saving actions on their behalf.[5] *Tōrah*, then, means God's will for human interaction and living *and* the human behaviors that accord with this will. Rather than a stricture that binds and limits, *tōrah* is a lifestyle that frees, leads to the deepest happiness, and generates blessing for all in the community.

Living the way of *tōrah* is not easy, however, for in this world the way of the righteous is often hidden or belittled, while the way of the unrighteous is overt, enticing, and applauded. Many psalms will remind us that choosing the way of righteousness will lead us head-on into confrontation with those who prefer the way of unrighteousness. If we choose righteousness, it is inevitable that the unrighteous will strive relentlessly to smack us down. After all, earthly turf is at stake. We need only look at the lives of persons such as Oscar Romero, Dorothy Stang, Martin Luther King Jr., and all the saints who have walked before us. We need only ponder our own lives when we make hard decisions to speak an uncomfortable truth, to stand up for justice, to put in an honest day's work when others scoff at such behavior. The reality in this world is that the righteous will struggle with the wicked until the end of time. There will be no rest for us on the journey. Yet Psalm 1 makes the eschatological promise that those who choose not to stand with the wicked now will stand like tall trees on the day of judgment (v. 3). The wicked, on the other hand, will be the ones unable to stand (v. 5)—rootless, they will simply be blown away like worthless chaff (v. 4).

A further quandary presented by Psalm 1 is its claim that for those who choose God's way, "whatever they do prospers" (v. 3), yet how often the opposite seems to be so. How often, as in Psalm 73, do we cry out in envy of the luxuries, ease, and success of the wicked whose lifestyle spares them the burdens of the righteous?

> But as for me, my feet had almost slipped;
>   I had nearly lost my foothold.
> For I envied the arrogant
>   when I saw the prosperity of the wicked.

[5] Bernhard W. Anderson, *Out of the Depths: The Psalms Speak for Us Today*, rev. and expanded ed. (Philadelphia: Westminster, 1983), 220.

They have no struggles;
>   their bodies are healthy and strong.
They are free from common human burdens;
>   they are not plagued by human ills. . . .

This is what the wicked are like—
>   always free of care, they go on amassing wealth.
>   (vv. 2-5, 12)

These persons mock the way of righteousness (v. 1) and, while they will be blown away like useless chaff at the end of time, they are certainly enjoying the world's pleasures, powers, and protections now. Again, the problem arises because of our feeble attempts at English translation of Hebrew notions. We tend to think of "prosperity" only in economic terms. A prosperous person is successful in business affairs and wealthy in physical possessions. But the prosperity to which meditation on the *torah* leads is "shalom" (Heb. *shālôm*), that societal condition in which all members of the community have what is needed for life, sustenance, peace, and well-being. Prosperity does not have to do with power or possessions but with the equitable use of these for the good of all. From this viewpoint a businessman who loses his company to bankruptcy because he turned all his profits, even his personal savings, into just wages for his employees is truly prosperous. A hospital aid who works long hours for little wages because she chooses to give the best care and compassion to the sick and the suffering in her midst is accruing the most valuable wealth. Who, according to Psalm 1, will stand up for all eternity?

From Journey's Beginning to Journey's End

Just as Psalm 1 was placed deliberately at the head of the Psalter, so was Psalm 150 placed deliberately at its end. Psalm 1 invites us to take up a "spirituality of pilgrimage and journey"[6] and sets before us the "itinerary of behavior"[7] that is to map our way. Psalm 150,

---

[6] Jean-Pierre Prévost, *A Short Dictionary of the Psalms* (Collegeville, MN: Liturgical Press, 1997), 74.

[7] Terrien, *The Psalms*, 77.

on the other hand, does not teach us about the way but celebrates our arrival at its ending. This hymn is one long shout of joy that through all the tribulations and temptations of the pilgrimage of faithful living, God has seen us through to the end! God has brought us to our appointed destiny and oh, how glorious it is!

For Walter Brueggemann, the very *canonical shape* of the Psalter asserts the *shape of life* lived by the covenant.[8] As the Psalter's bookends, Psalm 1 and Psalm 150 reveal the pilgrimage of faithful living to be a journey through obedience to praise.[9] Our steadfast following of the way of God moves us slowly but surely "from commandment to communion," "from *willing duty* to *utter delight*."[10] We become the way we walk, we become like the God who walks with us, we become God's "Alleluia!"

---

[8] Walter Brueggemann, *The Psalms and the Life of Faith*, ed. Patrick D. Miller (Minneapolis: Augsburg Fortress, 1995), 193; italics in original.

[9] Ibid.

[10] Ibid., 195, 196; italics in original.

PART II

The Psalms Shape Faith

The following four chapters draw on the work of two scholars in particular to shed light on the message and meaning of the psalms for the church today. The first is V. Steven Parrish, whose creative and thoughtful *A Story of the Psalms: Conversation, Canon, and Congregation*[1] looks at the Hebrew Psalter as a theological retelling of the story of the Israelites from their emergence as a nation through their demise under Babylon to their reemergence as a new people with a transformed understanding of and faith in the God of the covenant. The second is Walter Brueggemann, whose essays collected in *The Psalms and the Life of Faith*[2] offer challenging insights into the role the psalms play in the formation of faith both for Israel of old and for the church of today.

Chapter 3 summarizes Israel's salvation history from the exodus of their release from Egypt to the new exodus of their release from captivity in Babylon, and examines how the psalms recast this story in the theological framework Israel needed after Babylon to

---

[1] V. Steven Parrish, *A Story of the Psalms: Conversation, Canon, and Congregation* (Collegeville, MN: Liturgical Press, 2003).

[2] Walter Brueggemann, *The Psalms and the Life of Faith*, ed. Patrick D. Miller (Minneapolis: Augsburg Fortress, 1995).

reshape its faith in the God of salvation and the promises of the covenant. Chapter 4 looks more deeply into the faith shaped by Israel's praying of the psalms, and explores how our praying the psalms today forms this same faith in us, the community of the church. Chapter 5 uses questions raised by Walter Brueggemann to ponder the depths and intricacies of faith in a God who is personally engaged in human life and history: Who is the "You" addressed in the psalms? Who is the "I" who makes this address? What does it mean for this "I" to address this particular "You"? What happens to the "I" who makes such an audacious address? Chapter 6 contemplates how the story and the faith of Israel is the story and the faith of Jesus. How was Jesus himself formed by praying the psalms? What faith experience did the psalms shape in him? How in praying the psalms today do we, the church, conform ourselves more fully to who we are: the Body of Christ believing, living, and loving as Jesus in today's world?

The Psalms
Interpreted Israel's Story

Israel's Story

We Christians of the twenty-first century might easily assume that the Israelites of the exodus experience arrived quickly and readily at a fully formed faith in the one God who was Lord of all and giver of salvation. However, the case is actually quite different. As they journeyed those forty long years in the desert they struggled with belief and trust in this God who had revealed the divine Self first to their wandering forebears Abraham and Sarah, and more immediately to their leader Moses by way of a strangely burning bush. Despite the many interventions of this God on their behalf (the plagues in Egypt, the destruction of Pharaoh's army in the torrential waters of the Red Sea, the feeding of their shrunken bellies with miraculous manna from heaven, the quenching of their thirst with water gushing from dry rock), the Israelites squandered most of their energy whining about the hardships of their desert journey and against the God who had led them into it. Many times God—and if not God, then Moses—wanted to be done with this tiresome people (Exod 32:7-10; 33:3-5; Num 14:11-12, 26-35). Many times the people wanted to be done with God (Exod 16:2-3; also Exod 17:2-4; 32:1-6; Num 14:1-4).

Yet God persisted in moving them forward. They arrived at the promised land flowing with milk and honey, and made it their own. Once settled and prosperous, however, they again whined, this time for a king who would make them look like other tribes and nations. God relented, but with a double proviso: I alone will remain your true King, the one alone who can save you from death and destruction, the one alone to whom you are to give allegiance; and I alone shall be the one to appoint your earthly king (see Ps 2:6), who shall be as a son to me (see 2 Sam 7:14; 1 Chr 17:13; Ps 2:7), who shall extend my rule of justice and righteousness over you (see 1 Sam 9:15-17; 10:1; Deut 17:18-20). Thus Israel became established as a kingdom with a monarchy. Under David, the greatest of its kings, Israel grew in might and prosperity. The community remained boldly confident that this situation of power and prosperity would maintain, for, after all, was this not what God had promised? "Your house and your kingdom shall be made sure forever before me; your throne shall be established forever" (2 Sam 7:16; also see 2 Sam 7:18-29; 1 Chr 17:7-14; Ps 89:3-4, 19-37).[3]

But such bold confidence with its assumption of a safe and secure future proved to be naive indeed. The books of 1 and 2 Kings record the egregious failure of Israel's monarchs to act as God's envoys among the people, dispensing God's justice to the poor and God's judgment to the unrighteous. Repeatedly, they abandoned this mission in favor of self-aggrandizement and personal profit. They became oppressors of the weak rather than their protectors, shepherds who fled when the enemy attacked, leaving the people scattered and defenseless (Jer 23:1-2). In turn, the people themselves abandoned the ways of God; moreover, they showed no remorse for doing so (Jer 44:10, 23). Jeremiah railed against their infidelity and warned of consequences to come, but no one paid heed. In a devastating denouement the land was invaded, the temple destroyed, and the people carried off into exile (2 Kgs 25:1-12; Jer 39:1-14; 52:4-16), where they wept and wondered over what had happened to them. What has become of us and our homeland? they cried. Where is our promised prosperity? Where is the God who called us into being as a special people and then

---

[3] Scripture verses in this chapter are taken from NRSV.

swore protection and perpetuity to our king? Can we ever again trust in this God?

Only through a long and painful experience of dissolution and disillusionment did the faith of Israel reemerge. God intervened again, inspiring King Cyrus to release the Israelites from captivity and return them to their homeland (2 Chr 36:22-23). What they found on their return, however, was devastating: their land was a barren waste, their temple an ash pile, and their community a mere remnant. As the books of Ezra and Nehemiah report, it would be a long and painstaking process before the temple was rebuilt, the land restored, and the returned exiles reforged as a people. Israel would reemerge, but without a monarchy and as a dispersed people who must pilgrimage yearly to Jerusalem in order to maintain their national identity and reaffirm their covenant relationship with God and one another.

Israel's story does not end here but this telling covers the distance retold in theological terms by the psalms edited and organized into the Hebrew Psalter. The editing and organizing of the Psalter was an intentional response to Israel's experience of exile in Babylon, to her loss of land, monarchy, and temple, and to her ensuing faith struggle with a God who seemed to have reneged on promises made. The Psalter is divided into five books (Pss 1–41; 42–72; 73–89; 90–106; 107–50) and one hears in them "voices that remember the emergence of Israel, the establishment of monarchy, the collapse of monarchy, and the re-emergence of Israel."[4] One also hears Israel's faith struggle. The Psalter retells this story and this struggle in the light of covenant faith. Interpreting the past, the Psalter envisions the future and sees both held in the hands of God.

The Psalms' Interpretation

V. Steven Parrish explores how each book of the Psalter is its own chapter in the retelling of the story of Israel. The narrative begins with a prologue (Pss 1 and 2) that foretells the tension that will

---

[4] V. Steven Parrish, *A Story of the Psalms: Conversation, Canon, and Congregation* (Collegeville, MN: Liturgical Press, 2003), 6.

mark Israel's struggle to remain faithful to the demands of the covenant. Psalm 1 offers a choice between two ways of life, one righteous, the other unrighteous. Those who choose righteousness will be rewarded. They shall be like trees planted near water that bear plentiful fruit and never wither. The wicked, on the other hand, will perish like chaff blown away in the wind. Happy indeed will be those who delight in the law of the Lord and make this law their way of life.

Against this promise Psalm 2 slams the reality of the way things really are in this world. The powers that be will conspire to the death against the ways of God. God will prevail and the unrighteous will perish, but in the meantime the righteous must find their way in the midst of a pitched battle. Happy will they be who take refuge in God; happy will they be who maintain faith.

Immediately on the heels of the tension set up by Psalms 1–2 comes Psalm 3. Its inscription tells the tale: "A Psalm of David, when he fled from his son Absalom." David, in Psalm 2 named God's son and promised victory over any and all enemies, is in Psalm 3 pursued not by rogue nations but by his own son seeking to destroy him. How quickly the dynasty appointed by God has turned upon itself. Yet David maintains faith: You, Lord, are my shield; I am not afraid, for you—and you alone—will bring deliverance (see vv. 3-8).

Books 1 and 2 of the Psalter present Israel already under a well-established monarchy. The Psalter does not begin with the exodus journey, nor even with the call of Abraham, although it will refer to these pivotal events many times as the foundations of Israel's faith. The Psalter opens with Israel already well-settled in the promised land and the Davidic dynasty well-enthroned. The psalms in books 1 and 2 focus intensely on David (fifty-five of the seventy-two allude to him in their superscriptions). Clearly, for Israel David epitomizes the ideal king, both in the past and for the future. The overall theme of these initial books is that the monarchy merits "legitimation and maintenance."[5]

---

[5] Ibid., 51.

This is evident in the royal psalms (psalms about the king), which appear in these books. Psalm 18 portrays David as faithful without fault (vv. 20-24) and, because of this, protected from overpowering enemies by an even mightier God. Psalm 19 depicts a David who cherishes God's law and begs God to keep him free from fault. Like the beginning of Psalm 18, the conclusion of Psalm 19 addresses God as rock and savior. David knows where he stands and upon whose shoulders. David is the king *par excellence* who knows who he is before God and who he is to be before the people: the prime keeper and enforcer of God's law. The Psalter juxtaposes Psalms 18–19 to remind Israel of this intimate connection between kingship and Torah.[6]

Psalm 45 sounds the high note of the voices raised in favor of the monarchy. This poem is not addressed to God but to the king himself and his bride-to-be. This king is handsome to behold and unassailable in character. The poet promises to make him famous forever (it is significant that the "I" here making this promise is not God, but a human being, perhaps, we might conjecture, the court-appointed musician?).

Psalm 72 closes books 1 and 2 with this line: "The prayers of David son of Jesse are ended" (v. 20). Psalm 72 is a prayer that God give the king justice and righteousness, long life and dominion, wealth and blessings. The psalmist asks for such divine gratuity with great confidence because the king has been faithful to his role as emissary of God's compassion for the poor and intervener on behalf of the needy (vv. 12-14). The psalmist also clearly acknowledges that the authority and the righteousness of the king are God's doing (vv. 18-19). Indeed, this psalm "holds out high promise for the society ruled by the right kind of king."[7]

But these psalms lauding the monarchy are countered by voices raised elsewhere against it. Books 1 and 2 of the Psalter must be read concomitantly with the historical books of 1 and 2 Kings, which depict in graphic detail a monarchy that is not all it is cracked up to be. Despite the high claims of Psalms 18 and 72, king after

[6] Ibid., 56.
[7] Ibid., 61.

king from Solomon onward abandons the mission to be God's justice and righteousness among the people. The poor are distraught,
the prophets go unheeded, and the kingdom is tottering.

Book 3 of the Psalter addresses the collapse of Israel's monarchy. The book begins with Psalms 73 and 74 raising perplexed
and painful cries to God who, in seeming disregard of the promise
of Psalm 1, is allowing the unrighteous to flourish and the faithful
to perish. Despite the inclusion of three psalms (Pss 76, 84, 87)
expressing certainty in God's continued presence in and rulership
from the nation's center Jerusalem/Zion, the book concludes by
lamenting the demise of the Davidic dynasty and the seeming
vacuity of God's promise that David and his offspring would rule
forever (Ps 89).

Psalm 73 stands as the "theological center of the Psalter."[8] The
psalm begins with God's promise to reward the upright (v. 1), then
describes with seeming incredulity the wealth and good fortune en-
joyed by the wicked (vv. 3-14). Envious, the psalmist finds himself
tempted to slip from the path of righteousness (vv. 2-3). Wearied
by the struggle, he enters God's sanctuary, where he receives the
gift to discern that the ones truly slipping are the unrighteous (vv.
15-20). The psalmist has meditated on the law of the Lord and
come once more to delight in it (see Ps 1).

Faithfulness is vindicated and trust in God renewed. "[Y]ou,"
the psalmist prays, "hold my right hand. / You guide me with your
counsel . . . [You are] the strength of my heart and my portion
forever" (vv. 23-26). Thus in a nutshell Psalm 73 relates the whole
story of Israel's salvation: God's covenant promise of blessing and
prosperity, God's seeming failure to make good on this promise,
the ensuing temptation to abandon fidelity to God, and the discovery after a deeper look at things that the promise is in fact being
fulfilled, both now and in the future. With restored faith and quiet
confidence the psalmist resumes walking in the way of God.

---

[8] Ibid., 82, citing Walter Brueggemann, "Bounded by Obedience and Love: The
Psalms as Canon," in *The Psalms and the Life of Faith*, ed. Patrick D. Miller, 204–13
(Minneapolis: Augsburg Fortress, 1995).

Nonetheless, book 3 immediately raises a contrasting voice in Psalm 74. The confident assertion of Psalm 73 that God "hold[s] my right hand" is replaced in Psalm 74 by the cry, "O God, why do you cast us off forever?" (v. 1). The sanctuary, which in Psalm 73 provided the place where the heart was strengthened and commitment renewed, is burned to the ground in Psalm 74 (vv. 3-8). "Why," O God, "do you hold back your hand" (v. 11) you once offered us? the psalmist cries. Verses 12-19 recite God's mighty acts of creation as prelude to the punch line of verses 18-23: Remember, God, your covenant; forget not the poor and the downtrodden; forget not "your [own] cause." The Israelites challenge God to act according to who God has revealed the divine Self to be. They maintain faith in the face of disaster and destruction by calling on God to maintain faith by being the savior God has promised to be.

Psalms 76, 84, and 87 punctuate book 3 at various points. Classified as psalms of Zion, these poems depict Jerusalem as the place of God's sovereignty over all nations, as the locus of dispensation of God's judgment over all peoples, and the place of God's dwelling where the faithful find happiness and blessing. These psalms pose a countering voice to that of Psalm 74, which depicts the destruction of God's dwelling place. Some scholars view the Zion psalms as eschatological promises to be fulfilled in some distant but certain future, inserted in book 3 of the Psalter to give Israel hope in the midst of destruction. Others believe these psalms were composed after Israel's return from Babylon and celebrate the rebuilding of the temple. Parrish proposes a third interpretation. He suggests Psalms 76, 84, and 87 represent voices attempting to deny the reality of the current political and cultural situation with its rumblings of imminent demise. These are voices whistling in the dark in a last-ditch effort to distract the community from hearing the locomotive barreling down the track on which they so blithely stand.[9] The more telling voices are those of Psalms 73–74 and 88–89, which open and close this chapter in Israel's history. Set as the framework for book 3, these psalms move the community

---

[9] Parrish, *A Story of the Psalms*, 85.

from assurance and renewal found in the sanctuary, to destruction of the temple, to denial that this could ever happen, and finally to reluctant acknowledgment that this is in fact what has come to pass.

Psalm 88 deserves particular attention, for it stands alone in the Psalter as the only individual lament that does not conclude with a word of hope. The psalmist is stripped of everything, cast off even by God, abandoned by all human associates, attended only by darkness. From the individual cry of Psalm 88, book 3 moves to the lament of the entire nation in Psalm 89. Verses 19-37 acclaim the divine promise that David's dynasty would last forever; verses 38-51 describe the demise of this dynasty. Verses 1-2 acclaim God's steadfast love and faithfulness; verse 49 asks where this steadfast love and faithfulness have gone. On both counts, what once seemed undeniable has become unbelievable.[10] What has happened, the psalm asks, to the Davidic dynasty? What has happened to God's promise that this dynasty would last forever and that through it Israel would always have power, place, and prosperity?

Thus book 3 is framed by the pained voices of Psalms 73–74 and 88–89, which disclaim the voices of naive praise found in Psalms 76, 84, and 87. It is these voices of lament arising from realistic acknowledgment of a desperate and defunct situation that open the door to the possibility of salvation. Moreover, they open the throat to the possibility of real praise for the One who alone can and does save.[11] Only voices that name pain and feel the absence of God can pronounce a praise that is authentic.

Books 4 and 5 function as a unit. Their remembrance of the past goes further back than the promises made to David and their vision of the future goes further forward than the restoration after Babylon. Their remembrance of things past acknowledges the losses this past has brought and identifies the cause of those losses as Israel's own infidelity. Out of this brutally honest assessment arises a hope that is no naive whistling in the dark but an open-eyed and long-range vision of God creating new life out of decimation and death.

[10] Ibid., 92.
[11] Ibid., 94–95.

Book 4 opens with the only psalm in the Psalter attributed to Moses: Psalm 90—"A Prayer of Moses, the man of God." The man of the hour (or more precisely, the man of the ages) acclaimed in books 1 and 2 to be David is here acknowledged to be Moses. With this attribution the editors of the Psalter make an intentional return to the time of Moses when there was no land, no temple, no monarchy but only a wilderness, a promise, and a God revealing Self in "powerful and foundational ways."[12] Psalm 91 is partner to Psalm 90. Together they acknowledge human frailty and God's eternal sufficiency. After Babylon these two texts "point the way that a different Israel in a different wilderness will have to take."[13]

This way follows the route of an array of psalms proclaiming the sovereignty of God over all creation and all history (Pss 93 and 96–99). Psalm 89 articulated the dilemma in which Israel found itself: Where was the steadfast love God had sworn to David? How had they who were God's chosen ones become a destroyed people? What had happened to them? And what was the meaning of the faith they had placed in God? To this stressed and doubting frame of heart and mind Psalms 93, 96–99 raise the assured shout: God reigns! Psalm 93, for example, proclaims that God is in charge and does so without denying the real chaos that surrounds and threatens human existence. The psalm testifies that God is more powerful than this chaos. Psalm 96 announces a "new song" sprung of hope grasped in a newer, deeper way because it has known the fires of pain and loss. The shout "God reigns!" is not wishful thinking but "the faithful affirmation of a reality that slowly and powerfully takes hold."[14] The future Israel staked in the monarchy had not panned out; indeed, blind faith in this monarchy had brought Israel to its destruction. Together with Psalms 90–91, Psalms 93, 96–99 reshape Israel's faith by calling the community to remember a more distant past and to discover in that past that their "future

[12] Ibid., 106.
[13] Ibid., 108.
[14] Ibid., 109.

would lie in the relinquishment of [their] claims of autonomy and self-rule and [their] ultimate trust in the creator of all the earth."[15]

Psalm 105 draws Israel back to these earliest memories. The psalm retells the marvelous deeds of God on behalf of Israel from the promise made to Abraham through the exodus to the fulfillment of that promise in the possession of the land. In this psalm God remembers the covenant, but it is the one established with Abraham, not the one made with David. Moreover, in this psalm God is the subject of almost every verb. It is never Israel who acts.[16] This literary device communicates first that it is God alone who saves: no human being, no human institution, no human culture or code can do this. Secondly, the device communicates that Israel has yet to say how it *was* acting during the unfolding of this story. The language of the psalm places God squarely on the throne. By "decentering" all other powers, Psalm 105 recenters God as the One who alone reigns over history.[17] What is missing from the language sets up the significance of and necessity for Psalm 106, the final voice of book 4.

Written during the Babylonian captivity, Psalm 106 voices loud and clear that the demise of the Israelites was the consequence of their own behavior. At long last the Israelites acknowledge their complicity in what had happened to them: they were carried off into exile because of their own choice to abandon the covenant. With Psalm 106 the community openly confesses its sin: "Both we and our ancestors have sinned; / we have committed iniquity, have done wickedly" (v. 6). How opposite this is from the assertion of David in Psalm 18 that he has never departed from God's law but always stood blameless. The issue here is not David as an individual, but David as the monarchic representative of the whole community. Read as bookmarks placed respectively near the beginning and the ending of the Psalter, Psalm 18 and Psalm 106 show how far the community of Israel has journeyed in self-knowledge,

15 Ibid., 113.
16 Ibid., 119.
17 Ibid., 129.

shifting from protestations of absolute innocence to honest and open confession of infidelity.

Psalm 106 also proclaims that the God who has forgiven and saved this people in the past will forgive and save them now. Time and again this people has forgotten God and God's ways (vv. 13, 21). But God never forgets the covenant and, remarkably, always shows compassion on this people's weaknesses and wanderings (v. 45). The psalm reviews the moments in Israel's history—the crossing of the Red Sea, the testing of God in the desert, the building of the golden calf, the numerous infidelities in the promised land—when this recalcitrant people were saved by God in spite of themselves and articulates at last what they have taken so long to understand: that in every event of destruction or death God was acting for their salvation. Psalm 106 voices the new and transformed faith born of hard experience, honest self-assessment, and divine steadfastness.

Book 5 is the longest in the Psalter. In it the laments that formed the predominant genre in books 1–4 are replaced by psalm after psalm of praise and thanksgiving to the God who lifts up the lowly and hears the cry of the poor. For Parrish these psalms are "about *the possibility of movement*—physical, social, psychological, and theological."[18] The songs of ascents (Pss 120–34), for example, move the people forward on their yearly pilgrimages to Jerusalem, the central symbol of their reemerged faith and the place where they regularly renew their covenant relationship with God and one another. These same psalms move the people forward in their understanding of their true center, the God who sits enthroned in Jerusalem and who heals every ill and restores every broken heart. Psalm 150 stands as the goal and end point not only of the Psalter but of the whole story of Israel, indeed of the whole history of humankind. In Psalm 150, with joyful abandon Israel shouts one Alleluia after another in praise of the God who creates, sustains, and redeems, forever and ever, Amen!

---

[18] Ibid., 121; italics in original.

4

The Psalms
Transformed Israel's Faith

Read in juxtaposition with the history of Israel, the psalms reveal how the Israelites struggled with their faith in the God of the covenant, especially when it seemed this God was not being faithful to the covenant promises. The real issue, of course, was not God's infidelity, but Israel's. The psalms tell how the chosen people gradually came to terms with this truth and in so doing redefined their understanding of God, of themselves, and of the covenant.

The psalms reveal the itinerary of Israel's faith journey. Even more, the very praying of the psalms enabled Israel to traverse this journey. What movements in faith and self-understanding did the chosen people experience? What did they learn about faith and their covenant with God along the way? How did the praying of the psalms help them express what they were learning and move them forward? Finally, how does *our* praying the psalms *today* take us on this same journey and form us in this same faith?

Israel's Movement Forward

Every journey involves movement that is psychological as well as physical. For the Israelites, the physical journeys from slavery to the promised land, from this land to captivity in Babylon, and from captivity back to their homeland generated enormous shifts in their internal geographies. Over and over they were forced to redefine themselves and their relationship with the God who had called them into being and promised them prosperity and perpetuity. Over and over they had to replace false theology, false hope, and a false interpretation of events and reality with the truth of God. To do so they had to grapple with a recurring problem of denial: denial of how bad things really were (for example, that the monarchy was crumbling and disaster imminent), denial of their own culpability for their situation, and denial of the anger and distrust they felt toward God, who seemed to be reneging on the divine promises made to them. Facing their denial and coming to a new understanding entailed several shifts in thinking and believing.

One shift was that the community gradually relinquished their reliance on human resources and acknowledged their absolute dependency on God. Over time they came to understand that God alone reigned over nature and history. To affirm God alone as creator and savior meant removing any other power or individual from this position. To center belief and hope in the God of Abraham and Moses, Israel had to "decenter" its false gods, be they the pagan gods of its neighbors or the self-installed god of misplaced confidence in its own monarchical system of governance. The learning was a hard one. It took generations of bad rule and the final destruction of the nation by the Babylonians for the people to acknowledge that one king after another had abandoned the covenant, ignored God's law, and become the oppressor of the poor rather than their protector. It took years of exile in a foreign land followed by a long and arduous return and recovery for the people to acknowledge their complicity in what had happened to them. Recentering their faith on God alone and acknowledging the duplicity of their accusation that God had been the unfaithful one required a stupendous shift away from self-centeredness. Bottom line, they had to acknowledge that they were creatures and by definition limited, finite, and prey to repeated misrepresentation of self. They could never be the source of their own salvation. But God could be and ever was. Israel had to replace every false expectation that salvation could come from human culture or achievement and trust in God alone as the source of salvation.

Concomitantly, the Israelites amended their interpretation of the events of history. The community learned to look beneath the surface of events to discern what was really going on. They looked deeper into the past and further into the future, discovering over and over that what at first glance appeared to be death was in fact the beginning of rebirth. In fits and starts they realized that the death of the present way of being was necessary for a new and better way of being to take hold. Death—of the monarchy, of the nation, of reliance on human control—was the doorway to the fuller and greater life God was offering. Natural disasters, political oppressions, military defeats were not calamities, then; they were the catalysts for God's redeeming action.

This, too, was a learning long in coming, a lesson in continual need of divine repetition. For to recognize the new beginning offered by God, Israel had to allow the death of both her false despair and her false hope. Throughout her history a faithful remnant in Israel maintained hope in God's promise of a future kingdom of justice and peace, fullness of life and freedom, sustenance and satiation, not only for herself but through her for all nations (Gen 12:1-3; 18:17-18). What needed continual amendment, however, was how this remnant understood the content and contours and the membership and mission of that kingdom, as well as how that kingdom would come to fulfillment.

Another shift was that the Israelites had to move from denying their culpability in the destruction they met at the hands of the Babylonians to acknowledging that their own sinfulness had brought about their disintegration. They moved from blaming God for their woes to admitting that these woes were the consequence of their own infidelity to the covenant. Without Jeremiah's condemnation of their infidelities, the Israelites would never have risen from the destruction of the Babylonian exile. Jeremiah forced them to face and name the truth that their own infidelity had led to their demise, not any unfaithfulness on the part of God. God's subsequent restoration, unmerited but graciously given, would lead Israel to repentance. This repentance would be the heart of Israel's renewal. The people would name their sins, weep over what they had done and the disaster their actions had wrought, and surrender themselves in new trust and hope to an unfailing and ever-forgiving God. Only then could they open themselves to receive the new world this God was offering.

What Israel Learned

As the chosen people underwent these shifts in understanding, they came to new insights about the nature of faith and the promises of the covenant. One thing they discovered was that faith necessarily engages human beings in a struggle with God. Such struggling faith only grows slowly, through trial and error, testing and repentance. But God remains constant, steadfast, and ever-patient.

Second, they learned that this faith struggle was expressed in and mediated by the political, cultural, and religious crises of historical time and place. God's interaction with the human community was not ahistorical; rather, God was acting in and through human history. Moreover, God always acted to save. For Israel the challenge of faith was to learn to interpret historical events of devastation, destruction, and death through the perspective of God's action in time and space. The community discovered that real history, especially its personal, national, and global tragedies, forced them to look more deeply into the meaning of faith, the necessity of fidelity to the covenant, and the content of their messianic hope.

Third, Israel learned to cry out to God from its anguish in time and space, either in acknowledgment of its sin and desire for conversion, or in mystification over the prosperity of the unrighteous, or in vengeful anger at those who caused it suffering. Israel learned that lamenting was necessary in order to overcome denial and admit the reality of death. Lamenting was necessary in order to reestablish hope in the God who would save from death.

Fourth, the Israelites learned to accept the necessity of death for salvation. Experience taught them that "when death is fully accepted, alternative modes of reality never before considered begin to come into focus."[1] Even more, faith taught them that God always

---

[1] V. Steven Parrish, *A Story of the Psalms: Conversation, Canon, and Congregation* (Collegeville, MN: Liturgical Press, 2003), 104.

acted through death to grant new and fuller life. In terms of their faith journey—paralleled in the geographic movements of Abraham and Sarah's departure from one homeland to another unknown one, in their ancestors' wilderness trek from Egypt to the promised land, in the remnant's return from Babylon to a once prosperous but now destroyed homeland—Israel learned that dislocation was not death, nor was death dislocation. Instead dislocation was simply movement from one place, one position, one moment of despair or loss or heartache, to a new position—be it spiritual or physical—of salvation. The impetus behind this movement through death to new life, whether recognized or not, was always God. When beginning anew was patently impossible, when the present situation held no potential for new life, God would bring about the impossible, the unexpected, the unwarranted.[2] God would always grant a new beginning.

Fifth, the Israelites learned that, in order to recognize God acting to save them, they must acknowledge their sins and infidelities. They must move from denial of personal culpability for their situation to honest assessment of themselves and their behavior. They must admit that God was not the unfaithful one, they themselves were.

Finally, the chosen people learned to trust in the absolute steadfastness of God toward them. They came both to know God and to understand themselves. They discovered what it meant to be lowly in the eyes of God, and in their lowliness to find themselves lifted up by the divine hand that had been acting in their favor since the beginning of history. Only in their lowliness could they cry out: You, Lord, are our redeemer; come and save us! Only in their lowliness could they let God be God.

How Praying the Psalms Moved Israel Forward

The prophets spoke the word of God to the community of Israel about the truth of their situation. The psalms cried out the word of the community to God about the situation. The psalms were the

---

[2] Walter Brueggemann makes this point repeatedly in *The Prophetic Imagination* 2nd ed. (Minneapolis: Augsburg Fortress, 2001).

way the Israelites named and spoke both the devastating depths of their suffering and the joyful heights of their covenant faith and trust in the God of salvation.

Psalms of Lament

Part of opening themselves to God meant embracing the necessity for full and unstinting expression of the anger, sorrow, and grief they felt when things did go wrong. Israel learned that to sing God's praise the community must first cry out its pain, that praise which is easy is also empty. Through her lamenting Israel verbalized how bad things were, and it was the very articulation of this pain and anger that opened the people's hearts to salvation. The incremental number of psalms of praise in books 4 and 5 of the Psalter was only possible because of the preponderance of psalms of lament in books 1 through 3. This movement from lament to praise set the Psalter on a decided trajectory. The endpoint would be Psalm 150, the litany of Alleluias to the God who creates, sustains, and saves.

Approximately two-thirds into book 5 of the Psalter stands a disturbing reminder of just how horrific the journey to faith and salvation had been for the community of Israel. Psalm 137 remembers Babylon and what the Israelites suffered at the hands of this enemy. In Babylon the community prayed never to forget Jerusalem (vv. 1-6); returned to their homeland, they now prayed that God never forget what had been done to them (vv. 7-9). Their prayer concludes by blessing those who will seek vengeance in the most horrifying and unimaginable way: "Happy shall they be who take your little ones / and dash them against the rock!" (v. 9, NRSV). Praying Psalm 137 taught Israel that authentic faith in the God of the covenant can deny neither the real evil that exists in the world nor the very real anger and vengefulness such evil engenders in its victims as well as its witnesses. Faith built on denial of such atrocities and such feelings is false faith. The praise of Psalm 150 raised without the anguish and anger of Psalm 137—or the despair of Psalm 88, the devastation of Psalm 89, and the penitence of Psalm 106—is empty praise. Only by praying such psalms of lament could the community name both their suffering and their sin and thereby come with fully open hearts to the God of salvation.

By couching calamity and destruction in terms that laid them at God's doorstep, laments such as Psalms 78, 80, and 90 enabled Israel to see the tragedies in its life as more than natural disasters or political events. Praying these texts helped Israel acknowledge that a larger, deeper, more pervasive divine force was shaping its future. Whatever happened, God was acting through it to draw Israel back to its identity as a chosen people called to righteous living.

The laments always moved Israel from groaning about its situation to expressing confidence in the God who would save.[3] In Psalm 116, for example, Israel speaks of itself as fettered by deadly chains and surrounded by the anguish of Sheol but also names God the protector of the innocent who will deliver from death. In Psalm 73 Israel discerns what is really going on despite the seeming prosperity of the unrighteous and recommits herself to covenant living and trust in the God who promises blessing to the righteous. Praying the laments moved the community from focus on self to recentering on the God who, despite appearances to the contrary, was moving them toward their promised messianic future.

Psalms of Praise

In their laments, the Israelites called God to be God by demanding: Come and set things right as you have promised. They were begging God to yield to them by being who God had revealed the divine Self to be. In their psalms of praise, however, they yielded themselves to God by proclaiming: You alone are Lord, you alone grant salvation. In their praising, they were letting God be God.[4]

Psalms such as 93, 96–99, and 105 celebrated God's sovereignty over all creation and all history. In these psalms Israel shouted: God

---

[3] The single exception to this is Psalm 88, which is the only individual lament not concluding with a word of hope.

[4] For more on lament as begging God to yield to Israel and praise as a way Israel yielded to God, see Walter Brueggemann, "The Psalms as Prayer," in *The Psalms and the Life of Faith*, ed. Patrick D. Miller, 54–57 (Minneapolis: Augsburg Fortress, 1995).

reigns! Without denying the real chaos surrounding and threatening human existence, Psalm 93 proclaimed that God was in charge. Psalm 96 announced the "new song" the community could sing because God had brought them through pain and loss to new life. Psalm 105 remembered the saving interventions of God on behalf of the chosen people from the time of Abraham, through the exodus journey, to the entrance into the promised land. Praying such psalms reshaped the community's faith by leading them to define their future in terms of their past, and to see in the convergence of memory and hope the continuous saving activity of God on their behalf.

Psalm 113 called Israel to praise God from the rising of the sun to its setting, for this was the God who watched over creation, raised the weak from dust and ashes, and granted fertility to the barren. Psalm 126 celebrated God's intervention in releasing the captives from Babylon and boldly begged God to act again in the same way. This was the Lord who did great things for the people; this was the Lord who enabled a people who sowed in tears to harvest in joy. Above all, Psalm 150 celebrated how well Israel had learned that the end of all history, of all experience, and of all prayer was praise of God who alone reigns and saves.

Praying these and all the many other psalms of praise transformed Israel's understanding of who God was: truly sovereign, truly savior, truly steadfast in fidelity. The psalms of praise also affirmed Israel's newfound understanding of who it was: the creature, the one in need of salvation, the one called to steadfast fidelity. With such awareness, the chosen people could venture into their future with unwavering confidence in its salvific outcome, for they were certain of who God was and at peace with who they were.

The Psalms and Our Journey of Faith

What are we to learn from Israel's faith journey? One learning is that we ought not to be surprised when we find ourselves resisting God. Like the Israelites, we will cling to false gods, false hopes, and false interpretations of reality as long as these offer us what appears to be life, and as long as what God seems to be offering us is death.

Another learning is that we ought not to be surprised that we must undergo continual conversion of heart and behavior to the ways of God and the ways of the covenant. Like the Israelites, we must name how much we count on physical prosperity or earthly powers or human wisdom to save us, and how often we make ourselves (or our bellies, or our bank accounts) our god. Over and over we must identify what the popular but false theology/hope of the day is and how we, whether through misguidance or misplaced hope or the malice of infidelity, fall prey to its attraction.

Finally, we learn that expressing without inhibition the anguish, anger, and sorrow we experience along the journey of faith is part of the conversion process. How often do we mistakenly think that faith requires the repression of such thoughts and feelings? Like the Israelites, we must learn that freely expressing such thoughts and feelings to God, even within a public forum, is necessary if our faith is to be authentic.

How does praying the psalms help us confront our false faith, describe reality truthfully, and move forward in the ways of God? For one thing, praying the psalms nudges us out of denial by forcing us to name realities we would prefer to ignore, feelings we would prefer to repress, and sinfulness we would prefer to keep hidden even from ourselves. Praying the psalms also forces us to confront the reality of death and in that confrontation to deepen trust in the God who conquers death. When we lament we acknowledge the limits of earthly experience, of human expectations, of self-fulfillment, of human power and control, of human fidelity, even of faith itself. We give our pain full expression so that we can experience it in the context of faith. When we praise we exult in the limitless power of God, in the unbounded reach of God's mercy, and in the indomitability of God's fidelity to us. We give our joy full expression so that we can experience the fullness of God.

Praying the psalms, then, frees us to be who we really are: human beings who struggle with faith and fidelity and who experience intense feelings, both positive and negative, about the God in charge of history. Such self-acceptance frees us to receive God for who God really is: the One who understands every human feeling and withstands any human recalcitrance because this God knows faith is a journey, that human stumbling is to be expected, and that the journey's salvific outcome is assured. Praying the psalms enables us to let God be truly God, ourselves be truly human, and our faith be truly authentic.

Walter Brueggemann states that "alongside language that *describes what is*, there is language that *evokes what is not*. Thus this language has a creative function. It does not simply follow reality and reflect it, but it leads reality to become what it is not."[5] The lived experience of the community of Israel shaped the language of the psalms, but the language of the psalms also transformed Israel's lived experience. The psalms have such decisive power because they not only express the inner state of the one praying them but they effect a change in that inner state. The language of the psalms mirrors both the world existing within the one praying and the world existing without, and reshapes both to fit its words and its meanings.[6] Moreover, the psalms effect this change precisely in their being prayed. While we listen to other texts of Scripture, we pray the texts of the psalms. And in praying them we truly hear them, from the inside out. For such power to be activated, we must pray these texts over and over, as did the community of Israel. Are we ready for such prayer?

[5] Brueggemann, "Psalms and the Life of Faith: A Suggested Typology of Function," in *The Psalms and the Life of Faith*, 26 (italics in original).

[6] For an excellent presentation of the sacramental power of the psalms to effect change within the one praying them, see Harry P. Nasuti, "The Sacramental Function of the Psalms in Contemporary Scholarship and Liturgical Practice," in *Psalms and Practice: Worship, Virtue, and Authority*, ed. Stephen Breck Reid, 78–89 (Collegeville, MN: Liturgical Press, 2001).

5

The Psalms
as Dialogue between YOU and I

This chapter continues our exploration of the transformative power of the psalms by contemplating the relationship between the "YOU" who is addressed in the psalms and the "I" who makes such address. We build from the work of Walter Brueggemann,[1] who looks insightfully at what it means to address God as YOU in the psalms. Who is this YOU we address? Just as there is no limit to who God is, so our answer to this question has no limit. We focus on only three aspects of God's self-revelation articulated in the texts of the psalms: first that God is intimately involved in human life and history, second that God is the source of salvation, and third that God offers us unlimited compassion and mercy.

We then take a look at the I who addresses the YOU of the psalms. It is not surprising that the texts of the psalms reveal this I to be acutely vulnerable to the vagaries of human existence, desperately in need of God's salvific interventions, and greatly in need of God's unrestrained mercy.

We conclude by exploring how the audacious address of the psalms—that this limited, vulnerable, and sinful human I can

---

[1] Walter Brueggemann, "The Psalms as Prayer" in *The Psalms and the Life of Faith*, ed. Patrick D. Miller, 33–66 (Minneapolis: Augsburg Fortress, 1995).

dare to call the invulnerable Lord of creation and ruler of history YOU—transforms our understanding of the world and redirects our behavior. Praying the psalms changes who we are by making us one with the very YOU we address and with all the other created beings in need of this YOU's care and compassion.

The YOU We Address

It is utterly amazing how often in the psalms we address God as YOU. We do not know the name of God, and yet we do: YOU. We cannot speak the name God, and yet we do: YOU. In the psalms the God who is beyond reach and beyond definition is totally and irrevocably approachable: YOU.

> And now, O Lord, what do I hope for?
> My hope is in you. (Ps 39:7)[2]
>
> What are mortals that you remember them?
> And human beings that you care for them? (Ps 8:4)

The psalms exude an astounding expectation on the part of those praying them that they may address the Lord of creation directly and intimately. The all-powerful Creator and Sustainer of the universe is not at the beck and call of natural forces, political powers, or pagan gods; yet this YOU places Self at the beck and call of the ragtag human clan with whom this same Self has established a very personal and very permanent covenant of love.

Who is this YOU of the psalms? Brueggemann points out that while God remains beyond definition or confinement, God is not "undifferentiated."[3] To begin with, this God is known and named as intimately present and related to the human story. This YOU recasts divine power and sovereignty as "urgent, determined solidarity"[4]

---

[2] Psalm verses in this chapter are taken from Joyce Ann Zimmerman, Kathleen Harmon, Jean-Pierre Prévost, and Delphine Kolker, *Pray without Ceasing: Prayer for Morning and Evening* (Collegeville, MN: Liturgical Press, 1993).

[3] Brueggemann, "The Psalms as Prayer," 39.

[4] Ibid., 44–45.

with all creation. Wherever Israel yearns for wholeness, God yearns;
whenever Israel grieves, God grieves.

> When I walk in the midst of distress,
>   you revive me against the anger of my enemies.
> You stretch out your hand,
>   and your right hand saves me;
> the LORD will do everything for me.
> O LORD, your steadfast love is forever. (Ps 138:7-8)

> All who take refuge in you shall rejoice;
> forever they will shout for joy.
> You will lay protection over them
> and all those who love your name
> will exult in you. (Ps 5:11)

> Who is like the LORD our God,
> enthroned above?
> Who looks down to watch over
> the skies and the earth?
> Who raises the weak from dust
> and the poor from ashes . . .
> Who brings home the sterile woman,
> now a rejoicing mother of many children? (Ps 113:5-9)

Second, God is known and named as the source of salvation.
Moreover, God's saving actions always surpass the expected and
the possible.[5] The psalms sing to the YOU who, when life has
been destroyed, righteousness thwarted, the hungry starved, and
the needy shunned, reverses the situation and brings salvation by
making the impossible happen.

> Come and see the accomplishments of God—
> an awesome work
>   on behalf of mortals.
> God turned the sea into dry land,
>   they crossed through the river on foot.

---

[5] Ibid., 40.

Therefore let us rejoice in God,
who rules over the world with power
and whose eyes watch over the nations. (Ps 66:5-7)

O LORD, you have brought my soul
   up from Sheol.
You have restored me to life. (Ps 30:3)

When the LORD accompanied
those who returned to Zion,
we were like dreamers.
Then our mouth
was filled with laughter
and our tongue with joy.
Then it was said among nations:
"The LORD has done great
deeds among these people." (Ps 126:1-2)

Above all, the God who saves acts repeatedly and consistently to right injustice, to protect the innocent, and to raise up the poor.

For you are not a God delighting in wickedness,
nor does evil daunt you.
Mockers cannot stand
before your eyes.
You hate all makers of emptiness,
and you will destroy speakers of deceit. (Ps 5:4-6a)

The LORD will be
a refuge for the poor,
a refuge in times of distress.
Those who know your name
will trust in you,
for you do not abandon those who seek you, O LORD. (Ps 9:18)

For you bless the righteous, O LORD;
as with a shield of delight you will crown them. (Ps 5:11-12)

Third, God is named and known as a fountain of infinite mercy. God laid the cornerstone of this self-revelation in the words spoken to Moses after the notorious incident in the desert of the golden calf. Importuned by Moses to relent of justified anger against the people for this infidelity, God proclaimed Godself to be "merciful and gracious, / slow to anger, / and abounding in steadfast love and faithfulness, / keeping steadfast love for the thousandth generation, / forgiving iniquity and transgression and sin" (Exod 34:6-7a, NRSV). Later, when the Israelites angered God again by whining that it would have been better to have died in Egypt than to face death in the desert, Moses threw these very words back in God's face. Moses first attempted cajolery to dissuade God from destroying the people: If you kill these people, he taunted, Egypt will claim it was because you were impotent to save them; do you really want this kind of reputation? Then Moses weighed in with this simple but effective plea: "let the power of the LORD be great in the way that you promised when you spoke, saying, / 'The LORD is slow to anger, / and abounding in steadfast love, / forgiving iniquity and transgression' . . . Forgive the iniquity of this people according to the greatness of your steadfast love; just as you have pardoned this people, from Egypt even until now." Hearing these words, God immediately relented and said, "I do forgive, just as you have asked" (Num 14:17-20, NRSV).

The Israelites would come to call these words the "little creed" and, following the lead of Moses, would freely and often pray them back to God:

> But you, O Lord, are a merciful and gracious God,
> slow to anger and rich in steadfast love and truth. (Ps 86:15;
>   see also Pss 103:8; 145:8)

Certainty of God's steadfast mercy would hold sway even when human beings would try to circumvent it. Jonah's attempt to escape his commission to preach repentance to the Ninevites, for example, is well known in the popular imagination; perhaps less recognized is his reasoning. What motivated his flight from God's command was his awareness of God's merciful nature. When the Ninevites repented and received God's forgiveness, Jonah angrily cried out, "O LORD! Is not this what I said while I was still in my own country? That is why I fled to Tarshish at the beginning; for I knew that you are a gracious God and merciful, slow to anger, and abounding in steadfast love, and ready to relent from punishing" (Jonah 4:2, NRSV). God proceeded to teach Jonah, and through him to remind Israel, that the divine will far exceeds any human desire or power. As Brueggemann puts it, God's costly solidarity does not always conform to our idolatrous self-intent. Ironically, by attempting to thwart God's forgiving nature Jonah unwittingly affirmed it.[6]

Amazingly, Israel learned this vocabulary that so positioned God in relation to the world from God's own mouth. On the earliest pages of the salvation story, God accosted history's first murderer, Cain, with these words: "Where is your brother Abel? . . . What have you done? Listen; your brother's blood is crying out to me from the ground!" (Gen 4:9-10, NRSV). In later chapters when the Israelites were suffering so abominably in Egypt, God declared to Moses, "I have witnessed the affliction of my people in Egypt and have heard their cry of complaint against their slave drivers, so I know well what they are suffering. Therefore I have come down to rescue them from the hands of the Egyptians and lead them out of that land to a good and spacious land, a land flowing with milk and honey" (Exod 3:7-8, NAB). As Israel prepared to enter the promised land, God established the norms of behavior expected of the community, commanding them to show particular care for the alien, the orphan, and the widow. "Remember," God admonished, "that you were a slave in the land of Egypt; therefore I am commanding you to do this" (Deut 24:19-22, NRSV).

This was the God Israel came to know through the course of her history. Moreover, the community of Israel understood that it was God's desire—even more, God's mandate—that they address their Creator and Savior as YOU. It was God who had initiated the covenant with them, God who had established them as a chosen and cherished people, God who had first addressed them as intimates. The Israelites would struggle with this understanding, for

---

[6] Ibid., 49.

it was beyond human conjecture. But they would also embrace it, and grow in both the delights and the challenges it would bring into their lives.

The I Who Makes Address

The Israelites also struggled with knowledge and acceptance of themselves as human beings. Their narrative of the first man and woman revealed an astute awareness of the built-in struggle human beings would have concerning who was to be in charge of history: the human self or God? Brueggemann proposes that the psalms' manner of addressing God as YOU was the corrective for this human tendency toward arrogance and false autonomy.[7] In the psalms the Israelites named the ruler of creation and of history YOU, called upon this YOU in times of dire distress and danger, and praised this YOU for unimaginable acts of salvation and deeds of power. Addressing God in this way established the right relationship between Israel and God: the divine YOU was surely in charge, yet this divine YOU was also intimately and actively involved in Israel's life. God was sovereign; yet God was also by choice interdependent with the community of Israel. As for the Israelites, they were totally dependent upon God for both existence and salvation, but also interdependent with God, collaborators in a covenant relationship directed toward the enacting of salvation.

Who, then, is the I of the psalms who cries out to the YOU? This I is the human being fully aware of his or her utter neediness and ultimate powerlessness. This I embraces and celebrates his or her total dependency on God.

> Turn your ear, O LORD,
> and answer me,
> for I am poor and needy. (Ps 86:1)
>
> O God, you are my God, I seek you;
> my soul thirsts for you.
> My flesh longs for you

---

[7] Ibid., 35–36.

in a dry and wasted land,
   deprived of water. (Ps 63:1)

This is the human being fully aware that salvation is beyond human capabilities and resources. This I begs for and rejoices in the saving interventions of God.

For you have delivered my soul from death,
   my eye from tears
   and my foot from stumbling. (Ps 116:8)

Do not hide your face from me;
      do not send your servant back in anger.
You are my help;
      do not let me go, do not abandon me,
      O God of my salvation. (Ps 27:9)

This is the human being fully aware of the need to bank on God's mercy and forgiveness, seventy times over. This I admits sinfulness and abandons self to a compassionate and redeeming God.

Be gracious to me, O God,
   in your steadfast love.
According to the abundance of your mercy
   blot out my transgressions.

Cleanse me completely from my guilt
   and purify me from my sin.
For my transgressions I do recognize,
   and my sin stands always before me. (Ps 51:1-2)

In praying the psalms, the Israelites were carrying their part of the interdependent bargain God had offered them. Their part can best be summarized as a yielding of self: the I giving self over to the YOU in acknowledgment of how lovingly and freely this YOU had first given Self over to I.

A Dialogue That Transforms

One of the points Brueggemann reiterates is that in the psalms Israel prays God's character back to God. Israel challenges God to be who God has named Godself to be: the YOU who works wonders; the YOU who brings about reversals and transformations; the YOU who surprises with the impossible; the YOU who is ever-righteous, steadfast in faithfulness, merciful and forgiving; and the YOU who always intervenes on behalf of the poor, the oppressed, and the suffering. To Brueggemann's point we add the insight that in the psalms God prays the divine character into us. By praying the psalms we become one with this YOU; we take on this YOU's consciousness, values, and visions. Most of all, we take on the costly solidarity of this YOU. When we choose to risk everything for this YOU as this YOU has risked all for us, we choose to risk everything for the human brothers and sisters, even enemies, for whom this YOU has given the life of his only Son.[8] In praying the psalms we become one with all of humankind: saints and sinners, believers and unbelievers, those at ease and those suffering unease, the poor and the poor in spirit, the hopeful and the despairing, the faithful and those struggling to be faithful.

We repeat a point made at the conclusion of chapter 4: the miracle of the psalms is that these prayers not only express the inner state of the one praying them but effect a change in that inner state. The texts of the psalms not only mirror the world already existing within the one praying but they also reshape that world to fit the words of the psalm.[9] The psalms play a sacramental role, for they are "the means by which the rest of Scripture is actualized in the believer. Indeed, they are not so much the human response to what is found in the rest of Scripture as they are the means by which such a response is made possible."[10]

The psalms effect this change precisely in their praying. While we listen to other texts of Scripture, we speak the texts of the psalms and in speaking these texts we truly hear them because their sound comes from within us. And what we hear from the inside

---

[8] Ibid., 65–66.

[9] See Harry P. Nasuti, "The Sacramental Function of the Psalms in Contemporary Scholarship and Liturgical Practice," in *Psalms and Practice: Worship, Virtue, and Authority,* ed. Stephen Breck Reid, 78–89 (Collegeville, MN: Liturgical Press, 2001).

[10] Ibid., 81.

out is the very identity of God responding to the very real cries of humankind. In praying the psalms we become God's self-revelation to humankind and humankind's self-revelation to God.

By praying the psalms the Israelites learned that they could not address the YOU of the story of salvation without implicating themselves in the story and without full confidence in the story's salvific outcome.[11] The same holds true for us. We cannot pray the psalms without surrendering ourselves more fully to God and without choosing to take on our part in the enactment of salvation. We cannot cry to God out of our poverty without becoming more actively concerned for the poor in our world today. We cannot beg God for mercy without growing in our capacity to offer our brothers and sisters this same mercy. In sum, we cannot pray the psalms without becoming one with the person of Christ, who in his flesh was the full self-revelation of God to humankind and the full self-revelation of humankind to God, the full yielding of God to humankind and the full yielding of humankind to God. Christ *is* the psalm, the song of God. In praying the psalms we who are his Body become more fully that psalm, that song.

[11] Brueggemann, "The Psalms as Prayer," 39.

6

The Psalms
as the Prayer of Jesus

Our reflections here are speculative rather than exegetical, for no one can fully know or understand the prayer experience of Jesus.[1] His easy familiarity with certain psalms indicates the importance they played in his prayer life.[2] But we cannot say the psalms shaped the faith of Jesus in the same way that we claim these prayers shaped the faith of Israel or form the faith of the church today. As the second person of the Trinity incarnated in human flesh, Jesus did not need his faith to be "shaped." His relationship with the Father was not based on something unseen yet still believed in. Rather, his very being was in full and constant communion with the Father: he knew the Father, he shared all things with the Father (John 16:5; 17:9-10), all that he had was given to him by the Father (John 15:15; 17:1). He and the Father were one (John 14:10-11; 17:21-22).

Yet in affirming Jesus' divinity we cannot minimize his humanity. As a human being, like us in all things except sin (2 Cor 5:21), Jesus

---

[1] Lucien Deiss, *When Christians Pray the Psalms*, trans. James and Monique Wilde (Franklin Park, IL: World Library Publications, 2005), 26.

[2] The gospels contain several examples of Jesus quoting certain psalms. For discussion of these examples and their meaning for Jesus, see Deiss, 18–27.

struggled with the reality of the human condition, both his own and that of the entire human community. He became tired, felt discouraged, was impatient with those who opposed his mission, and was worn out by his disciples' repeated inability to understand what he was teaching them. He faced fear on a level beyond what most of us will ever know, sweating blood as he prayed to be spared his passion and death. He knew what it felt like to be abandoned by God at the moment of his most intense need. To what extent—on a human level—did praying certain psalms give him hope, strengthen his confidence in the Father, and renew the courage he needed to continue his mission? To what extent did praying these psalms articulate his full participation in all that was human?

In the end, what we explore here is not so much how the psalms formed the faith of Jesus as how his praying of certain psalms might deepen our understanding of him, as well as our ability to pray these psalms with and in him. For Jesus prayed the psalms as the divine Son humanly incarnated. He integrated in his person both the human being crying to God out of every possible need and the full incarnation of God's merciful response. How does our praying the psalms deepen our union with Christ and form us in his consciousness, a consciousness at once fully divine and fully human? In other words, how does praying the psalms open us to deeper union with the Father, the Son, and the Spirit? And how does praying the psalms lead us to more compassionate relationship with our fellow human brothers and sisters?

This chapter is not an exegesis but a personal meditation. In the first section I reflect on the mystery of Christ as God become fully human. In the second section I describe a personal experience that has affected my praying of certain psalms, then share how this experience has opened up in me a felt sense of how Jesus might have prayed these psalms. Finally, I share how this development in my own praying of some psalms has helped me experience how praying the psalms forms us in the consciousness of Christ and enables us to become more fully his body lifting human need to the Father and his heart offering praise to the God who always responds in mercy and compassion.

The Mystery of Christ[3]

In the mystery of Christ we see fully and definitively that God simply could not stand at a distance. The God who said to Moses, "I have observed the misery of my people . . . I have heard their cry . . . and I have come down to deliver them" (Exod 3:7-8, NRSV) fulfilled this divine word with an unprecedented gesture of personal presence, disrobing Self of divine trappings and taking on human vesture (Phil 2:6-7). The Word became flesh.

By choice this Word completely descended into the poverty of human existence.[4] This was one meaning of Jesus' struggle with Satan in the desert. Satan wanted him to cling to his Godhead by exercising divine power over the limitations of human existence. "End your hunger with a miracle," Satan prodded. "Save yourself from falling to your death by a divine command; make me your god and grab the kingdoms of this world as your own." Instead Jesus "immersed himself in our misery and followed our road to the end. He did not escape from the torment of our life, nobly repudiating humanity. With the full weight of his divinity he descended into the abyss of human existence, penetrating its darkest depths. He was not spared from the dark mystery of our poverty as human beings."[5]

Fully divine, Christ knew from the inside God's vision for the world; fully human, he knew how wantonly human beings stumble instead in darkness. Like the prophets before him, Christ was driven not by anger at human beings, however, but by anguish over their plight, which he knew to be in some ways willfully chosen and in others unconsciously programmed.[6]

---

[3] This section is part of a presentation I gave at the 2005 Institute of Liturgical Studies at Valparaiso University. The full text, "Have We Come All This Way for Birth or Death? Liturgical Music as Prophetic Ministry," is available at http://www.valpo.edu/ils/assets/pdfs/Harmon_2005.pdf.

[4] Johannes Baptist Metz, *Poverty of Spirit*, trans. John Drury (Mahwah, NJ: Paulist Press, 1998), 7–12.

[5] Ibid., 12.

[6] In my remarks here about prophetic ministry I am indebted to Walter Brueggemann, *The Prophetic Imagination* (Minneapolis: Augsburg Fortress, 2001). See also

Like all prophets, Jesus saw what God intended the world to be and he saw how prevailing systems of alternative dreams and expectations generated a consciousness that co-opted this divine vision. Every culture, every language, every sociopolitical system, every religious ideology eventually and inevitably counters the vision of the kingdom of God with an alternative and enticing vision of its own. The people, poor and rich alike, oppressed and oppressor alike, haves and have-nots together become inebriated with a prevailing and saturating consciousness that counters the promise of the kingdom of God with the promise of an alternative satisfaction. Desperate for life, the people drink up. To appease hunger, we eat more; to overcome inadequacy, we spend more; to assuage grief, we seek revenge. Caught up in this prevailing consciousness, we fail to see the falsehood of its promises. Even more, in our frenzy to obtain these satisfactions we become blinded to the consequences our choices bear for the others who share this finite planet on which we live. We are unable to see that the more we eat, the less others have to eat; the more we spend on the frivolous, the less others have for basic sustenance; the more energy we put toward revenge, the less we have available for genuine justice.

The prophet weeps because he or she can see that the only way to salvation in this situation is through death. For the kingdom of God to break in, the prevailing consciousness that obstructs the coming of the kingdom must die. This dying will wreak great suffering for both the poor and the rich, the haves and the have-nots, those who are oppressed and those who do the oppressing. The prophet weeps because he or she sees that this suffering and death is not only inevitable but it is necessary. Only what is broken bleeds, and only what bleeds knows, from the inside, where life truly resides.

Two consequences result within the heart and mind of the prophet, consequences brought to their fullest expression in the actions of God-become-human, the person Jesus. The first is that the prophet loves not only the oppressed but also the oppressor.

---

my essay "Where Hearts Must Break: Pastoral Musician as Prophetic Minister" in *Pastoral Music* 28:6 (August–September 2004): 21–25.

Underneath the alienation eventually experienced by every prophet is a more pervasive and generative sense of connection with the community and with the God who wills from time to eternity the authentic well-being of every member of this community. Jesus' love for the oppressor was most fully revealed when from the cross he willed not revenge, but forgiveness. In his first appearance to the community of his disciples after his resurrection it was this forgiveness that he sent them into the world to dispense (John 20:21-23).

The second consequence is that the prophet realizes the death of the prevailing consciousness necessary for the coming of the kingdom of God will require the prophet's own death. Satan attempted more than once to talk Jesus out of this consequence, for the prince of darkness, the ultimate purveyor of every consciousness opposing the consciousness of God, knew that Jesus' descent into death would mean humanity's ascent into divinity. When his direct confrontation with Jesus in the desert failed, he hid a subsequent attempt beneath the love and concern of one of Jesus' closest friends, Peter (Matt 16:22-23). Jesus was not fooled, however: he named Peter for who he was ("Get behind me, Satan!") and called him to leave behind the false assurances of the prevailing consciousness and enter the mind of God. Immersed in the tradition of the prophets before him, Jesus knew that he could not lead the people where he had not first himself gone. Setting his face like flint (Isa 50:7), Jesus turned resolutely toward Jerusalem and the cross.

The prophetic ministry of Christ was summed up in the paschal mystery of this death and resurrection. On the cross the God who could not stand at a distance was experienced by God-become-human as utterly and ineffably absent. Jesus gave himself over completely to this experience, and in so doing fulfilled the Trinity's eternally held vision for humanity that our relinquishing would be our gain, our death would be our resurrection. Into this broken, bleeding heart of Christ God poured new life. And the unexpected, the unbelievable, the impossible happened. This new life did not seep away through the broken heart's cracks but mended this heart into a new vessel capable of pouring blood and water out to the farthest reach of the cosmos and down into its smallest nooks and crannies.

A Personal Experience

In 2005 Sr. Dorothy Stang, a member of my religious congregation who labored among the poorest of the poor in the Amazon region of northern Brazil, was murdered by hired assassins. For thirty years Dorothy had championed the rights of the dispossessed as well as the necessity of protecting the Amazon rainforest for the well-being of the earth. Her work placed her in increasing opposition to big-business ranchers and loggers who repeatedly displaced the poor farmers by burning their crops and destroying their homes, and who chopped down huge swaths of the forest for their own gain.

Despite many direct threats to her life, and with full cognizance that her name was on the death lists drawn up by the ranchers and loggers, Dorothy chose to stay with her people. She told us it was not her life that counted but the lives of the poor who were struggling to sustain themselves and the land on which they lived. On the day before her death, Dorothy walked the mud road to a settlement that had just been burned to the ground, on her way to gather the people, to comfort them and pray with them, and then to organize them for rebuilding. That evening she spoke to the two men who had been hired to kill her, knowing full well who they were and what they were about. Unable to talk them out of what they had determined to do, she raised her hand in blessing over them, and went to bed. Early the next morning, February 12, the two men approached her on the last leg of her walk to the burned compound. As the first drew his gun and pointed it at her, Dorothy reached into her cloth bag and pulled out her Bible. "I have no gun. The only weapon I carry is this," she said. Opening her Bible, she began to read to them, "Blessed are the pure in heart, for they shall see God. Blessed are the meek, for they shall inherit the earth. Blessed are they who hunger and thirst after righteousness . . ." They shot her six times. Her body fell to the ground, her blood mingling with the rain and the mud. She was dead instantly.

I had never before known a martyr. I had never before shared stories and laughter with a fellow sister who would one day lay down her life for the poor. I had never before embraced at the sign of peace before Communion a body that would one day lie in its

own sacrificial blood. And I will never again pray Psalm 5 without
hearing Dorothy's voice praying it:

> Give ear to my words, O LORD,
> perceive my groaning.
> Be attentive to the sound of my cry,
> my Sovereign and my God,
> for to you I pray.
> O LORD, in the morning
> hear my voice.
> In the morning I prepare for you
> and I keep watching.
>
> For you are not a God delighting in wickedness,
> nor does evil daunt you.
> Mockers cannot stand
> before your eyes.
> You hate all makers of emptiness,
> and you will destroy speakers of deceit.
> People of bloodshed and fraud,
> the LORD abhors.
>
> But I, in the abundance of your steadfast love,
> shall come to your house.
> With awe I shall prostrate myself in your holy temple.
> O LORD, guide me in your justice
> because of my adversaries;
> straighten your way before me.
>
> Nothing right comes from their mouths:
> their insides are rotted,
> their throats are open tombs,
> their tongues are forked.
> Prove them wrong, O God;
> let them fall by their own counsels.
> For their many transgressions,
> drive them away
> since they have rebelled against you.
>
> All who take refuge in you shall rejoice;
> forever they will shout for joy.

You will lay protection over them
and all those who love your name
will exult in you.
For you bless the righteous, O LORD;
as with a shield of delight you will crown them.[7]

I understand Psalm 5 in a way I never could have before. When I pray it now I hear Dorothy groaning for justice, hear her begging for God's guidance in face of death-dealing adversaries, hear her naming evil and evildoers for what and who they are. And I feel her clinging in faith to a God she knows will protect her beyond death and crown her with joy because of her love.

There are other psalms I also pray differently now because of Dorothy and the life she lived and the death she chose. Psalms 3, 27, and 36, for example, are all prayers of one who, surrounded by enemies, lifts a heartfelt cry to God and sings of God's steadfast love and protection. Another example, Psalm 131, expresses the peacefulness of one who has chosen contentment rather than pretentiousness, the simple rather than the grandiose, satisfaction with what has been given rather than restlessness for what has not. Dorothy was restless for justice and indefatigable in its pursuit, but in all other ways she was content with what she had and full of gratitude for it. She had made unlimited room inside of herself for what really mattered, God's people and God's earth.

The new entrance into praying the psalms that Dorothy's life and death have given me has also opened up for me a new sense of how Jesus might have prayed these psalms. When I pray Psalm 5, I hear not only Dorothy's voice, but also the voice of Jesus, and I enter through the psalm into his experience. What might he have felt as he spoke these words to his Father? What hope might these words have given him? What confidence in God's ultimate promise of protection and salvation? What courage to continue his mission? Now when I pray this psalm I encounter Jesus giving himself over

---

[7] Psalm 5 is taken from Joyce Ann Zimmerman, Kathleen Harmon, Jean-Pierre Prévost, and Delphine Kolker, *Pray without Ceasing: Prayer for Morning and Evening* (Collegeville, MN: Liturgical Press, 1993).

both to his Father in willing obedience to his mission, and to us human beings who are the reason for this mission. I have begun to see more clearly how in praying this and other psalms Jesus was choosing to enter more fully into what it meant to be human, and he was more fully incarnating God's merciful and salvific response to all that was human.

Taking on the Consciousness of Christ

What did Jesus know that Dorothy also understood and that the psalms mediate for our consciousness? First, no human power can guarantee salvation, happiness, or protection from destruction. In fact, human powers are often the forces that instigate destruction. God alone is our savior. Moreover, God is steadfast in love and unrelenting in the movement toward salvation. With God what appears to be death and destruction is merely a necessary step along the way to greater, fuller life, both for oneself and for the entire world.

Second, humanness is not to be feared or denigrated, but embraced. Being fully human is the pathway to salvation. Jesus chose to become human because he trusted what it meant to be human. He also distrusted what was human, knowing full well the darker regions of the human heart (John 2:24-25). But he did not flee from his humanity; rather, he offered it completely to his Father. Because he did so, his surrendered humanness became the sacrament of salvation for the world. Dorothy also surrendered her very humanness, in love for the poor of the Amazon, and in love for God who first loved so much that he gave the life of his own Son. Dorothy, too, knew full well the evil that lurked in the human heart and she chose to stand up against it for the sake of justice. She feared death, but she was able to face it head-on because of her love for God's people and her certainty of God's abiding love for her. This is humanness stretched to the full capacity for which God intended it.

Third, we must make a choice about how we are going to live out the life span given to us in the arena of human history. This is the choice outlined in Psalm 1, the decision to walk the way of righteousness. This choice must be made with full cognizance of the opposition it will generate and of the struggle the faithful person will experience maintaining trust in God's promise of blessing and prosperity when the unrighteous prosper and profit (see Ps 73). Jesus made the choice, as did Dorothy following in his footsteps. The choice for righteousness did not protect either of them from death, nor did it erase the very real fear each felt as this death approached. But certainty of God's steadfast love, of God's protection beyond death, of God's promise of glory for those who remain faithful to righteousness upheld them and gave them courage.

Finally, that abandonment of self is necessary for fullness of life. This is not an abandonment to an idea or ideal, but to a Person (three Persons, in fact). Jesus, and Dorothy in union with him, gave themselves over to God and God's will for humanity and the world. Their abandonment led to a death that was felt as total loss, even of God's presence and care. But it opened the doorway to a new and fuller life. Jesus and Dorothy staked their lives on God's promise that relinquishing all would open them to receiving even more. The cry of Psalm 22—"My God, my God, why have you abandoned me?"—would become for them the shout of Psalm 118—"I shall not die but live, / and declare the deeds of the LORD" (NAB).

From Dorothy to the psalms to Christ. From Christ through the psalms to the world. This has been my journey and it has been a great grace. It is resurrection already arising from the death Dorothy chose in union with Christ. Dorothy's life and death have enabled me to pray the psalms in deeper union with Jesus. In a manner that I had not previously experienced, I feel his presence, as I feel hers, when I pray them. And I want the consciousness these prayers articulate to flood my consciousness and transform my manner of living.

From the first moment of the incarnation Jesus was completely given over both to his Father and to his human brothers and sisters. Throughout the years of her life Dorothy grew in her ability to make this same gift of self. The psalms articulate in human terms this journey that begins with God's gift of Self to humankind and ends with God's completion of the work of our salvation. Praying them pulls us into the consciousness of the God who first loves

PART III

The Psalms Challenge Faith

Praying the psalms transforms our faith because these ancient prayers, born of the experience of Israel, open our hearts and minds to encounter God as God is, ourselves as we are, and salvation history as the narrative of God's saving work on our behalf. But these same texts also challenge our faith in God, in ourselves, and in the salvific undercurrent of human history.

The chapters that follow reflect on three of these challenges. The first is how to pray psalms with texts our contemporary minds find hard to understand. Some psalms jar us with outdated imagery, cosmology, or sociocultural practices. Other psalms confuse us with disjointed or incoherent texts. Do we pray these psalms as they are, setting aside our struggle with the confusing images, concepts, and discontinuities? Do we rewrite the offending verses, or simply skip them as we pray? Or do we do something in between?

The second challenge is what to do when confronted by the awesome, and awful, silence of God. The psalms are based on the conviction that God listens, yet how often does God seem not to be listening. Mysteriously and painfully for us, God withholds speech. Confronted by such divine silence, we are forced to relinquish our feeble, but persistent, efforts to control God. And this puts us in a dangerous position. We must face the void of God's possible absence. We must deal with the void of unknowing. We must enter the realm of death. Taking this step is never easy and, not surprisingly, we dig in our heels. The psalms shove us forward by persisting in addressing God even when God does not answer. How is such prayer in the face of divine silence an act of genuine and courageous faith?

The third challenge is what to do when the psalms force us to say words we do not wish to speak. Sometimes these words are about negative aspects of ourselves. Other times these words are about aspects of God we would rather not acknowledge. We would prefer polite conversation with God. The psalms, however, force us "to bring into our conversation with God feelings and thoughts that most of us think we need to get rid of before God will be interested in hearing from us."[1] They also force us to take a bold look at the wrath God rages toward those who are not faithful to the demands of the covenant, who malign the innocent, abandon the needy, mistreat the weak, and abuse power and wealth for their own gain. These are not comfortable psalms to pray. Do we omit them from our prayer? Or do we let them do God's work within us, and if so, how?

---

[1] Ellen F. Davis, *Getting Involved with God: Rediscovering the Old Testament* (Lanham, MD: Rowman & Littlefield, 2001), 5.

7

Dealing with Disconcerting Texts

Some psalms, such as Psalm 23, are easy to pray. Others, however, are plain difficult if not downright disturbing to pray. What are we to do with disconcerting psalm texts? Can we pray them? The disconcerting texts fall into various categories. In this chapter we look at two: psalm verses that can be off-putting because of obsolete references, and psalm verses that can be jarring because of a seeming discontinuity or incoherence with the rest of the text.

Dealing with Obsolete References

In Psalm 51 we pray that bulls might again be offered on God's altar (v. 21).[1] In Psalm 16 we swear not to participate in blood offerings with those who believe in false gods (v. 4), and we rejoice that God will not abandon us to Sheol (v. 10). In Psalm 75 God assures us that when the earth trembles "I have firmly set its pillars" (v. 4).

Some references like these can be understood by doing a bit of historical, cultural research. Animal sacrifice and blood offerings were typical religious rituals practiced by peoples during the time when the psalms were written. In Hebrew cosmology the earth rested on pillars sunk into the depths of the sea, and Sheol was the place beneath the earth to which the dead were consigned.

---

[1] Scripture citations and quotations in this chapter are taken from NAB.

Without knowledge of Hebrew religious practices and cosmology, these texts mystify us. Even with such knowledge, however, we cannot connect to these images in the same ready way as did the people who created the Hebrew Psalter. We simply live in another time and place and so our tongues can trip and our sensibilities stumble on these phrases.

In some cases, we can omit a historically or culturally obsolete term or image without loss of meaning. For example, the American edition of the Liturgy of the Hours (LH) eliminates the reference to bulls being offered on the altar at the conclusion of Psalm 51. A notable endorsement for this approach came from liturgist and Scripture scholar Lucien Deiss, who saw it as a way to facilitate the praying of this psalm by modern-day persons.[2]

On the other hand, there is a value to retaining such references in our praying of the psalms. Doing so grounds our praying in the historical trajectory of biblical faith. While we cannot bring to our praying of the psalms the cultural and cosmological mindset of the ancient Hebrew community, we can bring their mindset of faith in the one God who acts relentlessly for human salvation. Moreover, using these references leads to a more nuanced praying of a psalm that yields deeper insight into the faith of the chosen people. We can, for example, imagine a sacrificial offering symbolizing the complete gift of self to God. We can imagine God's hand holding the earth steady on quivering pillars. We can imagine a deep, dark place of the dead into which we pray God will never allow us to fall. Through such concrete images drawn from ancient Hebrew culture we can enter more fully into the religious experience of the Israelites and share more directly in the immediacy and the intensity of their faith in God.

Perhaps the best way to deal with this dilemma is to read the full text of a given psalm with several translations in front of us and

---

[2] Lucien Deiss, *When Christians Pray the Psalms*, trans. James and Monique Wilde (Franklin Park, IL: World Library Publications, 2005), 11. The Revised Grail Psalms (Conception Abbey/The Grail, 2010), which will become normative in future editions of the Liturgy of the Hours, restores the reference.

a good commentary or two in hand.[3] What insights emerge from studying the commentary(ies) and cross-referencing the various translations? How, in light of these learnings, might we best pray this psalm?

Dealing with Discontinuous or Incoherent Texts

In verses 1-9 of Psalm 63 we tell God how much we thirst for God, how divine love is better than life itself, how we cling to God all hours of the day and night. It is a jolt, then, in verses 10-12 to suddenly utter these words:

> But those who seek my life will come to ruin;
> > they shall go down to the depths of the earth!
> They shall be handed over to the sword
> > and become the prey of jackals!
> But the king shall rejoice in God;
> > all who swear by the Lord shall exult,
> > for the mouths of liars will be shut!

A love song to God has transmuted suddenly into a cry of vindictiveness against an enemy. What brought about this shift? Do these vengeful verses refer to some historical event in which the Israelites, under attack by an enemy, remained confident that God would defend and protect them and that with their king they would continue to rejoice in God? Is the reference generic, expressing trust that no destructive human behavior can separate Israel from its intimate relationship with God? Is it both generic and particular, a formula text to be prayed by an individual undergoing siege from, for example, a creditor seeking foreclosure on home and property, or a false accuser undermining a marriage, or an abusive employer threatening one's livelihood? At any rate, once we see that the

---

[3] For guidance in selecting translations and commentaries, see the introductory section of Jan Michael Joncas's essay "Psalms of Sorrow and Celebration," *Pastoral Music* 14:1 (October–November 1989): 29–33. Available online at http://www.npm.org/pastoral_music/issues/PM%20Vol%2014-1.pdf.

psalm is about holding God as the center of one's life and trusting this Center will hold under any and all duress, verses 10-12 not only make sense, but so does the structure of the psalm as a whole. In the face of some life-threatening enemy, the one praying—be it an individual or the Israelite nation as a whole—is telling God, who is their life's love, to get cracking about saving his or her life. This love song is a cajolery, and the one praying knows it will work.[4]

That said, it remains true that for contemporary Christians unversed in the cultural and religious context of Hebrew psalmody, praying the conclusion of Psalm 63 "cold" can be quite jarring. Two solutions present themselves. The first is to omit verses 10-12, as does the current Sunday Lectionary[5] and the current version of LH. The second is to retain the offending verses and do the hard work of educating ourselves about the content, context, and theology of the psalm.

The first option makes pastoral and liturgical sense for Sunday Mass where the psalm functions as commentary on the readings and gospel of the day. But it is perhaps not a good choice for LH, which is aimed at meditation on the psalms in their own right. In the context of LH, omitting these verses erodes the meaning of the psalm and robs us of the richness of the text as a whole. We miss the reason for the love song. We miss the tension that exists between hungering for God and dealing with real life situations that threaten our existence. Above all we miss the opportunity to enter into the confidence that allowed a faithful Israelite to cajole God so brazenly. In this psalm who is the one called to fidelity and obedience? Who is the one wielding power? And whose plan is this? The offending verses are indeed disconcerting, but what might LH gain if, having done some homework on the content, context, and theology of Psalm 63, we included these verses in our prayer?

---

[4] These insights are drawn from Thomas Peter Wahl, *The Lord's Song in a Foreign Land: The Psalms as Prayer* (Collegeville, MN: Liturgical Press, 1998), 9–12.

[5] Psalm 63 is used three times in the three-year Sunday cycle, is an option for All Souls, and is one of the eight common psalms that may be sung during Ordinary Time. In every case, verses 10-12 are omitted.

Another example of a disconcerting text in the psalms occurs in Psalm 95. As in Psalm 63, we begin Psalm 95 on an upbeat note, calling one another to come into God's presence with joyful noises and songs of praise. We then invite one another to kneel down before the God who made us and whose people we are. So far, so good. But then God speaks:

> Oh, that today you would hear his voice:
>> Do not harden your hearts as at Meribah,
>> as on the day of Massah in the desert.
> There your ancestors tested me;
>> they tried me though they had seen my works.
> Forty years I loathed that generation;
>> I said: "This people's heart goes astray;
>> they do not know my ways."
> Therefore I swore in my anger:
>> "They shall never enter my rest." (vv. 7b-11)

Have you ever been engaged in revelry brought to a sudden, shocked stop when some authority figure announces, "Listen up! You've got nothing to be dancing about here!"? This about sums up what happens in Psalm 95, and the change in tone will startle and discomfit anyone unfamiliar with the checkered history of Israel's journey to the promised land (the "my rest" of verse 11). Exodus 17:1-7 tells us the story of Massah and Meribah and how the Israelites whined against God and Moses because they were without water in the desert. God warns us not to assume we are beyond the turncoat behavior of our ancestors. Dance if you will, but maintain a sober awareness beneath your fancy footwork that what God really seeks is the joy emanating from a truly obedient life. Worship is empty if it comes from hearts focused on self rather than hearts given to God in trust and obedience.

The Sunday Lectionary uses verses from Psalm 95, including the imprecation of verses 7b-9, on four occasions. On the Third Sunday of Lent, Year A, the first reading relates the story of Massah and Meribah (Exod 17:3-7) and the gospel reading tells the story of the Samaritan woman at the well who listens to Jesus' words with her heart (John 4:5-42). In the escape from Egypt the Israelites had been given everything they needed by God and more. Yet at the first moment of hardship they whined bitterly against God, painting Moses as a charlatan who had led them into the desert to die of thirst. Paul tells us in the second reading that we, too, have been given everything we need and more: grace through Jesus Christ and the gift of the Holy Spirit (Rom 5:1-2, 5-8). Jesus asks the woman at the well, do you know "the gift of God"? The manner in which the woman only gradually discovers who Jesus is parallels our own progress in coming to recognize him and all that we have been given in him. We sing Psalm 95 to remind ourselves and one another that we can enter this process or we can close our hearts to it. We can cut it off when it does not meet our preconceived expectations, as did the Israelites in the desert, or we can stick with it no matter how challenging, as did the woman at the well. The choice is ours.

On the Fourth Sunday in Ordinary Time, Year B, the first reading challenges the Israelites to hear God's voice and heed what they hear (Deut 18:15-20), and the gospel reading relates the people's amazement at what they hear coming from the mouth of Jesus (Mk 1:21-28). The verses from Psalm 95 challenge us to hear the voice of God and raise the question each of us faces in our struggle with faithful discipleship: will we surrender to this authority? The truth is that, despite how good the news Christ speaks, many elements in our hearts resist. Psalm 95 pleads with us to remain faithful in our listening to God, yet knows well how real is the possibility that we may choose otherwise.

On the Twenty-Third Sunday in Ordinary Time, Year A, God tells the prophet Ezekiel in the first reading to speak words of warning to the wicked lest they perish (Ezek 33:7-9), and Jesus teaches the disciples in the gospel to handle sinfulness in the community by speaking directly to the one causing offense (Matt 18:15-20). Psalm 95 reminds us the human heart is fickle and easily hardened. We are called to hear the voice of God and heed it. But fidelity is not easy and so we are also called to confront one another honestly when we fail and to handle the conflicts and hurts among us directly and openly. We are to deal with our fickle, human hearts with the grace promised to us by Christ. At stake is the authenticity of our community and the genuineness of our worship.

On the Twenty-Seventh Sunday in Ordinary Time, Year C, when the disciples ask Jesus in the gospel to increase their faith, his answer about the servant being expected to do all the master commands even after having already done a great deal seems unrelated to their request (Luke 17:5-10). The first reading (Hab 1:2-3; 2:2-4), however, puts his answer in context. To have faith means to maintain hope in God's promise despite the long delay in its fulfillment. To have faith means to keep working at the task of discipleship even when we think that surely the task has been completed. To have faith means to keep trudging on to the promised land even when the going is rough and the goal far off. The first two strophes of Psalm 95 have us arriving at the goal with joyful song. The final strophe, however, reminds us we are still on the journey and that the temptation to give up faith and quit the task—as did many Israelites in the desert—is real.

In each use of Psalm 95 in the Sunday Lectionary, verses 7b-9 of the psalm are included because they shed important light on the faith journey of Israel, and on our own faith journey. To have omitted these disconcerting verses would have truncated the significance of this particular psalm as commentary on the readings of the day and as commentary on our Christian living. The final verses jar us because they are supposed to do just that.

LH uses Psalm 95 in its entirety, including verse 11 (1963 Grail translation), as the invitatory psalm for the beginning of Morning Prayer. LH places a heading before each psalm in its cursus to provide insight into the meaning and significance of the psalm for Christian living.[6] The heading provided for Psalm 95—"Encourage each other daily while it is still today" (Heb 3:13)—indicates the appropriateness of using this psalm as the invitatory. We are to begin each new day by praising and worshiping God. We are to begin each new day by entering God's presence with joy. But we are also to remember each new day how easy it is for the human heart to turn from God. Part of our daily prayer as Christians, then, is to pray for one another that we may remain faithful to listening to the voice of God and heeding what we hear.

---

[6] General Instruction of the Liturgy of the Hours, no. 111.

In the contexts of the Liturgy of the Word at Sunday Mass and the invitatory of LH, praying the discomfiting verses of Psalm 95 is essential to understanding the meaning and purpose of this psalm in Christian prayer and living. Here again the most appropriate way to handle a disconcerting psalm passage is to do the work of educating ourselves about the context and content of the psalm in question.

We have examined here only a small sampling of psalm verses that can be disconcerting to us modern-day Christians because they contain obscure, obsolete references or seem disconnected from, and even contradictory to, the surrounding text. We have suggested that some obsolete references can be omitted from our praying of the psalms without jeopardizing the meaning of the psalm. But we have also shown that some jarring verses cannot be eliminated from our praying of the psalms without destroying the theological meaning and spiritual implications of the text as a whole. This means we have work to do in terms of continuing to educate ourselves about the content of the psalms, the role they played in the faith life of the Hebrew community, and the role they play today in the life and prayer of the Christian community.

8

Persisting in Prayer when God Is Silent

We human beings cannot provide salvation for ourselves. In our search for fullness of life we are easily misled either by outside evildoers or by our own inside desires and weaknesses. The psalms teach us that God alone can save. Moreover, God is relentless in pursuing this goal. No infidelity on our part and no evildoing on the part of others ever stops God from reaching out toward us in infinite love.

There are psalms, however, that seem to indicate God has reneged on the divine promise of salvation and abandoned even those who are good and righteous. In these psalms the God whom we have been taught listens to every human prayer remains deathly silent. What role do such texts play in the prayer of Israel? What role do they play in the prayer of the church? How do we persist in addressing a God who is silent?

We begin by exploring in general the nature of psalms of lament, using Psalm 13 as our lens. Next we reflect on the text of Psalm 88, the one lament in the Hebrew Psalter that offers us no words of trust in God, no ray of hope, no way out of ultimate darkness. We explore how praying Psalm 88 is, despite appearances to the contrary, a transforming act of faith.

Psalms of Suffering: The Laments

The most frequently employed literary genre in the Hebrew Psalter is the lament. A lament typically begins with a cry to God for help.

Some unspecified evil, enemy, or disease threatens the one praying and he or she has turned to God for deliverance. Despite the frequency and intensity of the prayer, however, the one praying often complains that God is not listening, that God delays in answering. Nonetheless, the one praying remains certain of God's love and confident of God's ultimate intervention. Despite the psalmist's tenuous situation and God's seeming inattention, the lament always concludes with an expression of trust in God.

We see this progression from pain and complaint to praise and confidence, for example, in Psalm 13.

> How long, O LORD? Will you forget me forever?
>   How long will you hide your face from me?
> How long must I bear pain in my soul,
>   and have sorrow in my heart all day long?
> How long shall my enemy be exalted over me?
>
> Consider and answer me, O LORD my God!
>   Give light to my eyes, or I will sleep the sleep of death,
> and my enemy will say, "I have prevailed";
>   my foes will rejoice because I am shaken.
>
> But I trusted in your steadfast love;
>   my heart shall rejoice in your salvation.
> I will sing to the LORD,
>   because he has dealt bountifully with me.[1]

The words of the psalm are heartrending. The plaintive repetition of "How long," the cry that death will result if God does not answer, the expression of fear that enemies will triumph all communicate the direness of the psalmist's situation and the sense of abandonment by God he or she feels. Yet the final strophe sings with confidence and trust. Having trusted in God's love in the past, the psalmist knows he or she will rejoice in God's salvation in the future.

---

[1] Psalm verses in this chapter are taken from NRSV.

Psalm 88: Cry of Despair

In stark contrast, Psalm 88 ends in total darkness, offering no hope and no future. The one praying continually cries out to God: "at night, I cry out in your presence" (v. 1); "Every day I call on you" (v. 9); "in the morning my prayer comes before you" (v. 13). There is no break in the prayer. Yet God persists in casting the psalmist aside, hiding the divine face (v. 14). Even more painful, what is threatening the psalmist is not human enemies, or human evil, or disease, or debility. The psalmist's adversary is God:

> Your wrath lies heavy upon me,
>> and you overwhelm me with all your waves.
>
> You have caused my companions to shun me;
>> you have made me a thing of horror to them. (vv. 7-8a)
>
> Your wrath has swept over me;
>> your dread assaults destroy me.
> They surround me like a flood all day long;
>> from all sides they close in on me. (vv. 16-17)

As far as God is concerned, the one praying might as well be dead (vv. 10-12). The last verse of the psalm communicates how utterly cut off the psalmist feels: "You have caused friend and neighbor to shun me; / my companions are in darkness" (v. 18). No hope is expressed, no trust that God will ultimately intervene to save, no surety that even other human beings will act on the psalmist's behalf. The NIV translation captures this feeling of having been utterly abandoned by God even more eloquently: "darkness is my closest friend."

Psalm 88 is supremely disorientating for those who believe God listens to every cry for help. In this psalm God is not listening; even more disconcerting, God is the cause of the extreme suffering being undergone by the one praying. What are we to make of such a prayer?

To begin with, we need to recognize it as our prayer. The "dark night of the soul" is a real human experience spoken about by the mystics and experienced by every human being undergoing extreme physical, spiritual, or psychological duress. I am reminded of a friend admitted to the psych ward of a major rehabilitation center in the Midwest who told me she spent the first twenty-four hours curled up under a table in the hallway. In her darkness, all she could do was sing over and over, "Where are you, God? I am here, but where are you?" With understanding and compassion, another patient brought her a blanket and pillow, saying, "You're going to be under there a long time. You'll be needing these." I am also reminded of the Nigerian sister in my religious congregation who was kidnapped by revolutionaries, then beaten and brutalized for three days before being dumped barely alive on the side of the road. During those three days, her prayer could well have sounded like Psalm 88.

Even when the experience of the dark night is not ours person-ally, praying Psalm 88 unites our hearts and minds with all those, far or near, next door or across the ocean, sitting beside us at the family dinner table or scrabbling for food in Haiti, who are suffering such sense of abandonment by God. We become the prayer they cannot be at this time. And when we ourselves are in such straits, when we must struggle with the limits of life and the silence of God, Psalm 88 keeps us from running away from the experience by putting on our tongues the words we would rather not pray. For Scripture scholar Walter Brueggemann, "Psalm 88 stands as a mark of realism for biblical faith. It has its pastoral use, because there are situations in which easy, cheap talk of resolution must be avoided. Here are words not to be used frequently, but for the limit experiences when words must be honest and not claim too much."[2] In these limit situations, Brueggemann adds, "What we may not do is to rush to an easier psalm, or to give up on [God]."[3]

While Psalm 88 may appear to indicate loss of faith, then, it actually does quite the opposite. The very act of speaking to God when God does not respond is an expression of profound faith. The

---

[2] Walter Brueggemann, *The Message of the Psalms: A Theological Commentary* (Minneapolis: Augsburg Fortress, 1984), 81.

[3] Ibid., 80.

person who no longer believes would simply walk away, choosing to waste no more breath speaking to a God whose silence proves his nonexistence. For the Israelites who wrote the psalms, however, the failure of God to answer prayer did not lead them to doubt or atheism. On the contrary, God's silence led them to address God all the more intensely.[4] They couldn't do otherwise, for they knew they were a people who had been called into existence by dialogue with God. To stop speaking to God, even in face of cosmic silence on God's part, was to cease to be Israel.[5] Praying Psalm 88, then, was an act of faith in themselves as much as it was an act of faith in God.

Psalm 88 is what Brueggemann calls a psalm of disorientation.[6] These are the psalms we need when life has thrust us out of the comfort zone of safe, secure faith, when God is not in heaven and all is not right with the world. Psalm 88 provides us the words we need to address the disorientation to God. "And in that address something happens to the *disorientation.*"[7] In praying the psalm we speak the truth to the God of salvation. Even more, we speak the truth to ourselves, and the truth-speaking opens the doorway to our transformation. Our disorientation becomes, then, not a threat to faith but a passageway to more authentic faith. The very praying of Psalm 88 makes our disorientation a grace rather than a curse, a gain rather than a loss, life rather than death.

Recently, my children's choir was preparing to sing a choral setting of the following text found scratched on a cell wall in Cologne, Germany after World War II: "I believe in the sun even when it is not shining. I believe in love even when I feel it not. I believe in God even when he is silent." In preparation we spent some time talking about what the words meant. When I asked the children what experience or situation might lead someone to say "I believe in God even when he is silent," one of the third-graders immediately

---

[4] Ibid., 79.

[5] Ibid., 81.

[6] Ibid., 15–23.

[7] Walter Brueggemann, *Praying the Psalms: Engaging Scripture and the Life of the Spirit,* 2nd ed. (Eugene, OR: Cascade Books, 2007), 11.

responded, "When all your insides have drained out and it feels like you don't even have your soul left." She then dramatically slid off her chair into a lifeless heap on the floor. This child had never seen or prayed the text of Psalm 88, but she understood its content. She was not a child who had yet experienced in her own life the kind of extreme loss or pain that tests faith in God's presence and care. She herself had not yet heard the silence of God. Yet she could articulate from deep within her heart what this experience felt like. I credit the adults in her life, particularly her parents, who have taught her in ways spoken and unspoken what it means to be human beings who find grace in brokenness and faith in face of God's silence. This is the spirituality of the psalms, a spirituality that shaped God's people in the past, forms the church today, and will lead us into the future.

When the Psalms Make Us Say Things We Don't Want to Say

(or Maybe Do, but Don't Want to Admit It)

Perhaps the two most uncomfortable types of texts in the psalms are those that speak of God's anger, and those that express our desire for vengeance. Concerning God's anger, we prefer to focus only on God's kindness and mercy. Concerning our vengeful tendencies, we prefer to see ourselves as persons who have no such feelings or desires. The problem with regard to God is our application of humanlike qualities to the divine Being, but how else can we talk about God other than in the anthropomorphic terms we understand? The problem with regard to ourselves is just the opposite: we'd rather not have certain human feelings and tendencies and the best way to pretend we don't is never to voice them (at least not in polite company).

The psalms, however, are not polite in terms of either God or the human condition. Uncomfortable as the psalms voicing divine or human wrath may be, we have to deal with them as part of God's inspired word, as part of the prayer of the church, and as part of our growth in faith and discipleship.

Dealing with Psalms Expressing Human Vengeance

The place to begin coming to terms with human vengefulness in the psalms is the human condition. Whether we like it or not, violence perpetrated upon one human being by another is part of the stuff of life. And whether we like it or not, victims of violence desire vengeance.

During the 1960s I had a friend who was passionately committed to nonviolence and actively engaged in demonstrations against the Vietnam War. One evening she appeared unexpectedly at my door, distraught and agitated. "Last night my sister was attacked in her home, brutally beaten, and raped," she sobbed. "I've always told myself I was nonviolent, but when the police catch the man who did this, I'm going to beat his face to a pulp and tear his body apart, limb from limb!" She was not misconstruing her commitment to nonviolence, but discovering that her commitment had never been tested in the crucible of events close to her own life. She had never been a victim. She had never felt a desire for vengeance and come face-to-face with her own propensity for violent conduct. She found herself terrorized by and terrified of her feelings of rage. What was she to do?

It was the experience of the Israelites expressed in the psalms of vengeance that offered her a way forward. Here was a people who had suffered barbarity many times over, who had lived through the destruction of their homeland and way of life by the Babylonians, who knew the pathos of being scoffed at, belittled, oppressed, enslaved, and almost annihilated. Here was a people who felt a righteous desire for retaliation and who called upon their God to see it done:

> Break the arm of the wicked and the sinner!
> Pursue their wickedness till nothing remains! (Ps 10:15)[1]

> O God, break the teeth in their mouths;
> tear out the fangs of these lions, O LORD!

> Let them vanish like water that runs away;
> let them wither like grass that is trodden underfoot.
> Let them be like the snail that dissolves into slime,
> like a woman's miscarriage that never sees the sun.

---

[1] Psalm verses in this chapter are taken from *The Revised Grail Psalms* (Chicago: GIA Publications, 2010).

Before they put forth thorns, like a bramble,
let them be swept away, green wood or dry!
The just shall rejoice at the sight of vengeance;
they shall bathe their feet in the blood of the wicked.
    (Ps 58:7-11)

O daughter Babylon, destroyer,
blessed whoever repays you
the payment you paid to us!
Blessed whoever grasps and shatters
your children on the rock! (Ps 137:8-9)

Israel wrote these prayers as a way of coping with concrete experiences (both individual and communal) of violence, injustice, and oppression committed against them not only by enemies but also by friends and even family members. More important, God inspired Israel to compose these prayers of vengeance. God prompted the Israelites to give full expression to everything within their minds and hearts so that they could give all of it over to God's judgment and God's realignment. Only then could they turn from enacting vengeance to trusting that the Lord of time and history would ultimately set all human affairs aright. We see this change of heart, for example, in the juxtaposition of texts such as those already cited from Psalms 10, 58, and 137 with the following text from Psalm 11:

The LORD is in his holy temple;
the throne of the LORD is in heaven.
His eyes behold the world;
his gaze probes the children of men.

The LORD inspects the just and the wicked;
the lover of violence he hates.
He sends fire and brimstone on the wicked,
a scorching wind to fill their cup.
For the LORD is just and loves deeds of justice;
the upright shall behold his face. (Ps 11:4-7)

In Psalm 11 the Israelites move from chanting vengeance and wanting to dance in the blood of those who had done them wrong to handing the work of justice over to God. Having admitted their desire for revenge, they allow God to take over the action of setting things right. The important point here is that it was the *praying* of these psalms, the voicing of these texts, that brought about Israel's change in attitude. Praying the psalms of imprecation taught them to relinquish retaliation in trust that God would take care of it and would do so with far greater justice than they could bring to the task.

Such is part of the analysis Walter Brueggemann offers for the psalms of imprecation.[2] The Hebrew community who created the psalms never used propriety in prayer as a reason to back away from expressing ugly human sentiments. Instead, without edit, they laid bare before God exactly what was in their minds, hearts, and intentions. Such a *modus operandi* revealed how total was their trust in the God to whom they prayed. They felt no need to hide the less glorious dimensions of their personalities from the divine Being who had created them and entered into covenant with them as a beloved people. They trusted they could say anything to God and find not shock or revulsion, but acceptance and a hearing.

For one thing, this God already knows what possesses the human heart (as God become human attests in John 2:24-25). It is we ourselves who are oblivious about what resides beneath the surface of the persona we present to the world. The psalms of vengeance force us out of self-delusion by putting on our tongues those feelings, desires, and attitudes we would rather keep hidden from ourselves and others. Such open admission—confession—is the way we hand these sentiments over to God lest they take blind control of us. Praying the psalms of imprecation, then, is salvific, for it frees us to face ourselves honestly and hand over to God the demons we find there. Praying psalms of vengeance is an act of piety, for in such prayer we give ourselves over to God's redemptive work.

These psalms do not let us wiggle out of our own skin, but force us to live there, to acknowledge that the anger and vengeance present in the psalms are practiced in human life.[3] As Brueggemann

---

[2] See Walter Brueggemann, *Praying the Psalms: Engaging Scripture and the Life of the Spirit*, 2nd ed. (Eugene, OR: Cascade, 2007), chap. 5.

[3] Ibid., 64–65.

points out, "there is a way *beyond* the Psalms of vengeance, but it is a way *through* them and not *around* them."[4] We subjugate our capacity for hatred and revenge not by denying or disowning it but by accepting it as expected, understood, and human, and then handing it over to God to be redeemed.

Dealing with Psalms Expressing Divine Wrath

The psalms express not only human vengeance, however, but also the vengeance of God. This divine wrath is directed sometimes at the enemies of the faithful and other times at the faithful themselves.

> The Lord, standing at your right,
> shatters kings in the day of his wrath.
> He brings judgment among the nations,
> and heaps the bodies high;
> he shatters heads throughout the wide earth. (Ps 110:5-6)

> The LORD inspects the just and the wicked;
> the lover of violence he hates.
> He sends fire and brimstone on the wicked,
> a scorching wind to fill their cup. (Ps 11:5-6)

> How long, O LORD, God of hosts,
> will you be angry at the prayer of your people?
> You have fed them with tears for their bread,
> an abundance of tears for their drink.
> You have made us the taunt of our neighbors;
> our foes mock us among themselves. (Ps 80:5-7)

> Indeed, we are consumed by your anger;
> we are struck with terror at your fury. . . .
> All our days pass away in your anger.
> Our years are consumed like a sigh. . . .
> Who understands the power of your anger?
> Your fury matches the fear of you. (Ps 90:7, 9, 11)

[4] Ibid., 80.

What are we to make of such texts? Just as we grow in understanding psalms expressing human vengeance by considering the human condition, so do we come to understand psalms expressing God's anger by reflecting on the divine character.

One of the dominant themes about the character of God presented in the entirety of the Hebrew Psalter (and in all of Scripture) is this: God *intends* justice. Because of this divine intention, God takes angry action wherever that justice is lacking. God traps evildoers in their own plots (Pss 7:15-17; 9:16-17). God judges against those who terrorize others (Ps 10:18). God makes those who "eat up my people as if eating bread" tremble with fear (Ps 14:4). God rises up "for the poor who are oppressed and the needy who groan" to "grant them the salvation for which they long" (Ps 12:6). The psalms make clear that God simply will not tolerate injustice, oppression, and the affliction of the powerless by the unrighteous powerful.

Furthermore, the psalms (as all of Scripture) make clear that God *demands* justice from human beings. When human beings defile the dignity and rights of one another, when the poor remain powerless because of the manipulation and deceit of the powerful, when the innocent are crushed, God calls the human community to task, as in Psalm 106:

> They poured out innocent blood,
> the blood of their sons and daughters,
> whom they offered to the idols of Canaan.
> The land was polluted with blood.
>
> So they defiled themselves by their actions;
> their deeds where those of a harlot.
> Then God's anger blazed against his people;
> he was filled with horror at his heritage.
>
> So he handed them over to the nations,
> and their foes became their rulers. (Ps 106:38-41)

Typical of the psalms that express God's response against injustice, Psalm 106 uses anthropomorphic terms. Horrified at the behavior of the chosen people, God blazes with anger. The people who created the psalms simply had no other way of conceptualizing the reactions of a divine Being who was beyond human knowing. What they did know were their own sensations of impatience, perturbation, anger, horror, and wrath. With poetic license they projected such onto God.

But with the psalms something more happens than the projection of human feelings and behaviors onto God. When we pray the psalms, God pours the divine character into us. To speak in prayer to God about divine horror at injustice is to feel God's horror. To speak to God in prayer about divine action on behalf of the poor and the oppressed is to take on that action in our own lives. The anthropomorphic language in the psalms does not cut God down to human size. Rather, it enlarges us to divine dimensions: we take on God's character and behavior.

While praying psalms expressing human vengeance moves us to relinquish certain behaviors (namely, acts of retaliation), praying psalms expressing God's wrath moves us to take up other behaviors (namely, acts of justice). Action for justice is very different, however, from action for retaliation, and it is the praying of the psalms that schools us in the difference. Praying the psalms transforms us into being persons who live the justice and righteousness of God.

Praying the Psalms of Vengeance

The preceding discussion leads to the conclusion that it is incumbent upon us to pray the psalms of vengeance. Praying them nonetheless remains uncomfortable. What are we to do? What follows are three options, each with merit, though not all equally meritorious.

Omit These Texts from Christian Prayer

In terms of liturgical prayer, the revised Liturgy of the Hours omits the extremely vitriolic Psalms 58, 83, and 109, as well as certain hate-filled verses in other psalms (General Instruction of the Liturgy of the Hours, no. 131). Lucien Deiss agrees with this omission, arguing that such texts are in disagreement with Christian values and teaching.[5] In terms of private prayer, we can choose to omit such texts on our own. But this must be done judiciously, for to forego all praying of psalms of vengeance is to shortchange our understanding and acceptance of ourselves as human beings and to foreclose on the redemptive work of God wrought through the praying of the psalms.

Reword the Psalms to Dispose of Disconcerting Texts

When Alan Gribben's edition of *The Adventures of Huckleberry Finn* appeared in 2011[6] with Mark Twain's 219 uses of the "N-word" in reference to African-Americans removed, intense debate ensued. Supporters of the excision argued that the book did no good if it sat dusty on a shelf, banned because of its language. Opponents argued that Twain had used this word deliberately to portray the cruel casualness with which blacks were dehumanized by whites in the post–Civil War period. The case is an example of a literary masterpiece from one historical period being "retranslated" to fit the political correctness of another. It is also an example of what happens to the power of a text when we eviscerate its language because we are uncomfortable with it. The challenge, of course, is to read the original masterpiece in context and learn from the juxtaposition of language and context how to act as better human beings.

The same is true of our reading and praying of the psalms of vengeance. To retranslate them so that all references to violence, anger, vengeance, retribution, retaliation, and hatred are removed is to destroy the power of these texts to make us honest about ourselves, to make our giving of self to God unabashed and uninhibited, to make us move from being persons who seek revenge to becoming persons who pursue God's work of justice.

---

[5] Lucien Deiss, *When Christians Pray the Psalms*, trans. James and Monique Wilde (Franklin Park, IL: World Library Publications, 2005), 33.

[6] Alan Gribben, ed., *Mark Twain's Adventures of Tom Sawyer and Huckleberry Finn* (Montgomery, AL: NewSouth Books, 2011).

Create Appropriate Situations for Praying Them

Carroll Stuhlmueller makes a creative and interesting suggestion regarding the imprecatory psalms. He agrees that omitting such texts from the regular cycle of the church's liturgical prayer is pastorally wise, but does not agree with our omitting them entirely from our consciousness. He would have members of the church gather deliberately at regular times during the year to pray the psalms of vengeance on behalf of those individuals and peoples so dehumanized by violence, torture, abuse, defilement, and oppression that they cannot pray.[7] The church must take on their cause and give them their voice. In doing so we take on God's cause. One fitting application of Stuhlmueller's suggestion would be to combine such psalmody, for example, with a modern-day Stations of the Cross during Lent.

At the time I originally wrote this essay, current news reports had been filled with the shocking story of a New York mother who piled her four children into her minivan and then deliberately drove it into the Hudson River. From across the country came the repeated cry, "How could a mother do this?" Those involved in investigating such incidents report, however, that across all classes, races, and socioeconomic levels, mothers murder their own children at a rate of one incident every three days. Experts argue that a contributing factor to this situation is "our reluctance as a society to believe mothers would be capable of killing their offspring."[8]

By contrast, the psalms teach us how to speak honestly about ourselves as human beings. The psalms teach us to pray without pretense. In the praying of the psalms we offer God the truth about ourselves. In response, God offers back the truth about the divine Self. And then this truth transforms us, without doubt the greatest sign that God is truly about the work of setting all things right.

---

[7] Carroll Stuhlmueller, *The Spirituality of the Psalms* (Collegeville, MN: Liturgical Press, 2002), 155.

[8] Jocelyn Noveck, "Mothers killing kids not nearly as rare as we think," *Dayton Daily News* (April 17, 2011): A23.

PART IV

Becoming the Psalms, Living the Spirituality

We began this book by sharing Joseph Gelineau's insight that one who prays the psalms becomes one of God's own psalms. We then asked what it means to become a psalm. We can now answer that it means one who prays the psalms, whether in private moments or liturgical celebrations, in quiet words or communal song, is shaped by the story he or she tells, and chooses to live out of that story. Throughout the preceding chapters we have articulated various aspects of the manner of living engendered by the praying of the psalms. We conclude this book with some summary insights gained as we have traversed this journey of reflection on the meaning and the power of the psalms. We look also at the important difference, and necessary relationship, between praying the psalms in private devotion and praying them communally as part of the church gathered for public worship.

Three Central Aspects of the Spirituality of the Psalms

The psalms as a collection reveal the faith journey of the Israelites as they came by fits and starts to discover the nature of the one true God and this God's love for them and desire to lead them to the fullness of life. Over and over during their history the Israelites would misconstrue their ultimate good, pursuing false gods and nearly destroying themselves in the process. Over and over the God who had made a covenant of everlasting love with them would pull them from the brink of destruction, forgive their wanderings from fidelity and righteousness, and refound them as a chosen people.

Beneath the checkered history of Israel's infidelity, then, runs the unbroken thread of God's fidelity to them and to the divine promise of salvation. Through this history Israel gradually came to learn who God was and who they were to be in relation to God and to one another as God's chosen people. They learned the paucity of their own power to save themselves, the weakness of their ability even to identify correctly the direction in which salvation lay (how often did they chase false gods and false hopes!). They learned utter reliance on the God of salvation and made the remarkable discovery that every infidelity on their part redounded not to their shame but to the glory of the God of infinite mercy and forgiveness.

As their faith experience unfolded, the Israelites created the psalms as poetic prayer texts expressing what they had come to know about God, themselves, and salvation. The psalms reveal, then, a spirituality specific to the experience of the Israelite community, a spirituality divinely inspired and humanly learned through all the ups and downs, trials and errors, joys and sorrows of salvation history as God revealed to them who the divine Self was, who they were, and how they were to live.

The spirituality of the psalms is multi-dimensional; here we identify just three of its central characteristics. First is the acknowledgment that as human beings we are utterly unable to bring ourselves to salvation. On the outside, we are surrounded by evildoers who demolish whatever is good, impede justice, and seek our destruction. On the inside, we are blinded by our own muddy vision of what is for our ultimate good and tripped up by our own repeated infidelity to God. Second is trust that God will be utterly faithful in bringing us to salvation. God is relentless in pursuit of us. No infidelity on our part and no evildoing on the part of others will ever stop God from reaching out to us in infinite mercy and love. Moreover, God's salvific concern for us is imbued with a compassionate understanding of us in all our humanness. Third is the discovery that salvation is nothing less than God's very gift of Self to us. Our part in the story is simply to give ourselves back, freely and fully.

It is in praying the Psalter as a whole that we discover these three central aspects of the spirituality of the psalms. But we also find all three of these components in a number of individual psalms. Psalm 31 is a prime example. Psalm 31 begins by placing us squarely in the middle of the unredeemed human situation: we need to be rescued; we are at risk and need to be saved; we need someone to be our rock of refuge. The psalmist already knows who this Rock is and gives self over in complete trust to this God:

> In you, O LORD, I seek refuge;
> > do not let me ever be put to shame;
> > in your righteousness deliver me.
> Incline your ear to me;
> > rescue me speedily.
> Be a rock of refuge for me,
> > a strong fortress to save me.
>
> You are indeed my rock and my fortress;
> > for your name's sake lead me and guide me,
> take me out of the net that is hidden for me,
> > for you are my refuge.
> Into your hand I commit my spirit;
> > you have redeemed me, O LORD, faithful God. (Ps 31:1-5)[1]

The psalm gives a dramatic depiction of the danger being faced:

> For I hear the whispering of many—
> > terror all around!—
> as they scheme together against me,
> > as they plot to take my life. (v. 13)

It also gives a poignant description of the effect this threat is having upon the psalmist: "my strength fails . . . my bones waste away"

---

[1] Psalm verses in this section are taken from NRSV.

(v. 10); "I am . . . a horror to my neighbors, / an object of dread to my acquaintances; / those who see me in the street flee from me" (v. 11). Yet the psalmist remains steadfast in trusting God:

> But I trust in you, O Lord;
>> I say, "You are my God."
> My times are in your hand;
>> deliver me from the hand of my enemies and persecutors.
> Let your face shine upon your servant;
>> save me in your steadfast love.
> Do not let me be put to shame, O Lord,
>> for I call on you;
> let the wicked be put to shame;
>> let them go dumbfounded to Sheol. (vv. 14-17)

The threat of destruction is not idle, nor is the psalmist's reaction in face of it placid, yet he or she trusts in the goodness and protection of God.

> O how abundant is your goodness
>> that you have laid up for those who fear you,
> and accomplished for those who take refuge in you,
>> in the sight of everyone!
> In the shelter of your presence you hide them
>> from human plots;
> you hold them safe under your shelter
>> from contentious tongues.
>
> Blessed be the Lord,
>> for he has wondrously shown his steadfast love to me
>> when I was beset as a city under siege.
> I had said in my alarm,
>> "I am driven far from your sight."
> But you heard my supplications
>> when I cried out to you for help. (vv. 19-22)

Finally, having given self over to God in complete trust, the psalmist calls all who know and love God to stand strong, courageous in the knowledge that God will protect those who are faithful and bring to justice those who do evil:

Love the LORD, all you his saints.
> The LORD preserves the faithful,
> > but abundantly repays the one who acts haughtily.
> Be strong, and let your heart take courage,
> > all you who wait for the LORD. (vv. 23-24)

Such is a powerful, transformative praying of Psalm 31. But such praying, done in private, is only one mode of our praying of the psalms. We also pray the psalms communally as part of the liturgy of the church. Praying the psalms liturgically, with the community of the church gathered for communal worship, is a different experience, and shapes a different response.

The Psalms as the Prayer of the Church

Sing to the Lord: Music in Divine Worship reminds us that "[t]he Psalter is the basic songbook of the Liturgy."[2] From the earliest days Christians sang the psalms when they gathered for worship. Today the church sings the psalms daily in the Liturgy of the Hours and in the celebration of Mass. What is it the psalms say that must be part of the prayer of the church?

The psalms tell the story of God's saving interaction with the human race. The church recognizes the fulfillment of God's saving work in the life, death, and resurrection of Christ. Christ is the fulfillment of the promise of the psalms because in his very person he incarnates the fullness of God's gift of Self to humankind and humankind's return gift of self to God. The church prays the psalms in the liturgy in order to enter as the communal Body of Christ into the self-giving of Christ. The church prays the psalms in order to become part of the story of salvation.

This is the reason, for example, that every year the church chooses to sing verses from Psalm 31 as part of the Good Friday liturgy of the Passion. In this psalm Christ shows us the way to salvation. He does this by taking on our humanity in all its poverty, standing

---

[2] *Sing to the Lord: Music in Divine Worship* (Washington, DC: United States Conference of Catholic Bishops, 2007), no. 115b.

powerless before sin and death. Stripped of everything, he can say but one prayer: "Father, into your hands I commend my spirit." In doing so he shows us that it is not human will and action that saves, but divine will and action. But he also shows us the role human will does have in salvation, for salvation is nothing other than the free, conscious, and complete giving of self over to the will of the Father. In this gift of self to God we become most fully human, and this is our redemption.

Sung liturgically as part of the Liturgy of the Word, Psalm 31 takes up a different voice from the one it sounds in our private praying of it. It becomes public proclamation of the word of God. Applied to liturgy, proclamation is a specific and unique kind of speech-act. It is not dramatic reading. It is not broadcast news reporting with all its hype and intensity. While dramatic reading and broadcast news reporting require training, they make no demands upon the one uttering the scripted words other than a certain level of technical skill. By contrast, liturgical proclamation demands commitment of self to God and God's way of being. It calls for transformation of life.

Proclaimed in the liturgy, the responsorial psalm is audible revelation of how the word of God has transformed the identity and behavior of the psalmist who is proclaiming that word. Authentic proclamation leads the gathered assembly to also make God's word their identity and their way of living. Together, proclaimer and assembly *become* God's word in a liturgical act of mutual listening, responding, and self-giving. When the psalmist sings the text of the psalm, she or he is proclaiming a conscious yes to what God is asking of her or him. When we sing our response, we proclaim our yes to what God is asking of us. That this yes is communal makes a difference—in fact, all the difference—in the world. In singing the responsorial psalm, we become the community God wishes us to be, we become the Body of Christ proclaiming his yes here-and-now in the world.

In our liturgical praying of the psalms we enter communally into the spirituality that shaped the life and mission of Jesus. We communally become fully human by taking on both the powerlessness of the human condition and the powerfulness of giving self completely over to God. We communally acknowledge human sinfulness and at the same time recognize every sin as a means for the triumph of God's mercy and forgiveness. We communally take on God's understanding of and compassion for all things human, and communally collaborate with God in the relentless divine pursuit of human salvation.

Whether prayed privately or communally within the liturgy, the psalms mold us in the way of God. The fact is, we need both modes of praying the psalms. The two forms are interdependent; each strengthens the capacity of the other to achieve its particular purpose in shaping our faith and forming our response to God. The one prepares us for the other. We cannot enter into the communal praying/singing of the psalms with understanding unless we have experienced the private praying of the psalms. We cannot undergo the full transformation to which the psalms call us unless we have experienced their communal praying in the liturgy.

Becoming the Psalms

We become the psalms, then, both as we pray them in private moments and as we sing them in communal liturgical celebrations. The psalms shape who we are as individuals and as members of the church. Even more, the psalms teach us that our individual identities are not separate from our communal identity: we are the church, the Body of Christ, part and parcel of one another, linked together in moving all of humankind toward the praise of God that transforms all lament.

The psalms shape who we are, individually and communally, because in praying them we are reminded over and over of the story of salvation and of the God who writes that story. We are lifted beyond limited self-understanding to a vision of our importance in the eyes of God who spares no effort on behalf of our salvation. We are stretched beyond self-absorption to a sense of identity with all of struggling humankind. We are immersed in the messy stuff of life and discover that we do indeed move from lament to praise. We are transformed in our beliefs and behaviors, and we begin to live a spirituality shaped by the psalms.

Through praying the psalms, we become persons who reflect consciously on how God is acting in our lives, and in the life of the world. We recognize the unfolding of salvation in ordinary events and experiences, and become able to tell the story of God's action on behalf of the world. We fear no human experience or emotion, positive or negative, because we know such to be the stuff out of which God will bring salvation.

We see God's handwriting everywhere. We see God's movement in all events, even moments of loss and grief, sin and pain, suffering and death, for we grasp the big picture—the end of the story already written into the beginning. We approach life with hope because we know that God's steadfast love, merciful compassion, and powerful justice are greater than any human sin or weakness, any natural disaster, any form of death.

We recognize the interconnectedness of all our stories, and strive to share this vision with others. We take time to listen to the stories of others, knowing that each one is a psalm, a story of divine-human interaction moving from lament and suffering to praise and thanksgiving. We pay compassionate heed to events in every corner of the globe, experiencing every cry of pain as our cry, every shout of jubilation as our shout. We exclude no one from God's embrace, and are actively engaged in the cause for justice and peace.

We offer God praise in every event of life, joyful or sad. We give thanks for all things great and small. We are confident of salvation and cognizant that it does not depend upon ourselves, and for this we give God thanks and praise.

When we pray and sing the psalms, then—whether alone or with others, whether in private prayer or gathered for liturgical prayer—we are praying and singing ourselves into being: being one with God, being one with all the community of the faithful, and being one with all of humankind. The psalms enable us to bridge the human and the divine, the individual and the communal, our lives engaged in worship and our lives busy with everyday tasks. In praying the psalms, we become the very embodiment of God's story of salvation. And we become this together, as the community of the church, the one Body of Christ.

St. Augustine tells us in his Exposition on Psalm 147, "Will you then sing a Psalm? Let not your voice alone sound the praises of God; but let your works also be in harmony with your voice. . . . To please then the ear, sing with your voice; but with your heart be not silent, with your life be not still."[3] Psalm 1 calls us to meditate on the way of God day and night. We noted in part I, chapter 2 of this present book that the Hebrew word for "meditate" (*hāghah*) means a kind of muttering or moaning, or a continuous whispering that, though quiet, is audible. The parallel word in English would be "murmur." Paradoxically, and surprisingly, the Latin root of "murmur" (*murmur*) means "to roar." May we, then, heed Augustine's admonition. May our praying of the psalms, our murmuring on the way of God, the ways of the human heart, and the way of those whose hearts are faithful to God, become a roar of hope and of trust, of lament and of praise, of justice and of joy. For the sake of the world, may our every thought, word, and deed become Christ's shout of "Amen! Alleluia!"

---

[3] St. Augustine, Exposition on Psalm 147, in *Nicene and Post-Nicene Fathers, First Series*, vol. 8, trans. J.E. Tweed, 2 (Buffalo, NY: Christian Literature Publishing, 1888).

Scripture Index